on garden design

In creating a garden, the design already exists.
It is hidden in the setting that man and nature have
   already provided,
and in the owner's taste and expectations.
The designer's skill is uncovering it.

KEITH CORLETT, *Spring 2004*

garden design
for small spaces
from backyards to
balconies to rooftops

Keith Corlett

STERLING PUBLISHING CO., INC.
NEW YORK

Library of Congress Cataloging-in-Publication Data
Corlett, Keith.
   Garden design for small spaces : from backyards to
balconies to rooftops / Keith Corlett.
       p. cm.
   Includes index.
   ISBN 0-8069-6411-1
  1. Gardens—Design. 2. Landscape gardening.
I. Title.
SB473 .C665 2004
712'.6—dc22

                                    2003025641

Library of Congress Cataloging-in-Publication Data

10 9 8 7 6 5 4 3 2 1

Published by Sterling Publishing Co., Inc.
387 Park Avenue South, New York, NY 10016
© 2004 by Keith Corlett
Distributed in Canada by Sterling Publishing
c/o Canadian Manda Group, 165 Dufferin Street
Toronto, Ontario, Canada M6K 3H6
Distributed in Great Britain by Chrysalis Books
   Group PLC
The Chrysalis Building, Bramley Road,
   London W10 6SP, England
Distributed in Australia by Capricorn Link
   (Australia) Pty. Ltd.
P.O. Box 704, Windsor, NSW 2756, Australia

Printed in China
All rights reserved

Sterling ISBN 0-8069-6411-1

FRONTISPIECE. *The Biblical Garden, at the Cathedral
Church of Saint John the Divine, in New York City.*

OPPOSITE. *A view from within the Biblical Garden.
The feeling of a full and complete garden can still be
achieved in a mere fraction of an acre.*

contents

introduction

as urban centers continue to grow, they bring about many changes in our lifestyles. With over three-quarters of the population now residing in metropolitan areas, living has become crowded and intense. With space evermore at a premium, we live cheek by jowl with our neighbors, as houses and garden sites become even smaller and closer together.

Despite this change in environment, however, gardening continues, almost paradoxically, to be the most popular hobby in the country. Perhaps the explanation is that the contrast of an oasis of green in an arid, concrete desert sharpens our senses and our appreciation of nature. Moreover, a garden provides refuge from the increased pressures of urban life and can be an inviting space to escape to.

But social changes and overcrowding present a major challenge. How can we create a full and complete garden in a small space that will capture the atmosphere we continue to want and—even more—need? Small backyards, patios, courtyards, and high terraces and balconies are much more common now than the spaciousness of an acre or two. The conventional approach to landscaping larger spaces does not address the problem of smallness. A different approach is required.

Overcoming this problem by using spatial illusion techniques when designing the small garden is what this book is all about. Through the use of scaled imagery, it is possible to make the small garden appear larger than it really is and, in so doing, retain the

Preceding page. Just like the towering backdrop of the buildings beyond, the upward growth habit of climbing roses—one of the many types of climbers—makes the best use of the vertical space. This compensates for the limited ground-surface planting area of the small urban lot.

Fig. i-1 (opposite). A scaled-down vine-covered shade pavilion can bring an unexpected sense of grandeur and feeling of spaciousness—one usually associated only with larger country estate gardens—to a small garden.

many pleasures and features generally associated with a larger space.

The idea of having a small garden is, of course, not new. The ancient Egyptians, Babylonians, Greeks, Romans, and other civilizations throughout history understood the pleasures of a natural retreat to soften the harshness of city or town living as urban centers grew and developed.

The Hanging Gardens of Babylon—one of the seven wonders of the ancient world and the most famous gardens of all time—are a prime example. They have long held a fascination for me. (They were called "hanging" because every part of the plant—roots, trunks, and foliage—was high above the viewers' heads.)

Built by Nebuchadnezzar II between 605 and 562 B.C. in the ancient empire of Babylonia (in Mesopotamia, where the Garden of Eden is traditionally considered to have been located), not only were they the finest and most imaginative example of how a garden could make living more pleasurable in a harsh, crowded metropolis, but their impressive grandeur was in keeping with the status of the largest city in the world at that time. Thought to have covered just under an acre, the Hanging Gardens were built in the form of a ziggurat (stepped pyramid). While a pyramid would have been the only structurally reliable shape, given the unstable nature of sun-baked mud bricks from which it was constructed, a ziggurat had the effect of more than doubling the surface area for plants and foliage relative to the ground space. It's not difficult to imagine the wonder expressed by travelers who might have been trekking across a vast arid plain for weeks or months before arriving. Of more importance to the modern small-space gardener is that not only did the Hanging

Gardens reflect the style and status of their owner, but that they
did so in a way that maximized the space available.

A blueprint re-creation of my idea of what the Gardens
might have looked like is shown in Fig. i-2. Although the
Gardens have never been found (the building material was very
vulnerable due to daily watering and, over time, to the periodic
flooding and course changes of the Euphrates River), in the
interest of authenticity, my blueprint design uses only archeological
artifacts and architectural styles of structures from that period that
still exist today.

A further blueprint of what a modern-day counterpart
to Babylon could look like is shown in Fig. i-3. It has individual

**Fig. i-2. Ancient Babylon—
the gardens were an important
site for hospitality as well as
relaxation.**

small gardens for many and common-area gardens for all, and it would be a perfect oasis for urban dwellers on high in the arid harshness of the city. If buildings for living continue to climb high, gardens should rise along with them. I see it as only logical and, given the advanced building techniques of today, well within the realm of possibility.

While such ambitious (perhaps even fanciful to some) examples are fine for stimulating the imagination and providing inspiration, today's more practical world of small-space garden design is the topic here, and this book contains a wide and varied assortment of achievable urban gardens at all levels. These range from backyards, courtyards, and patios to penthouses, balconies,

Fig. i-3. Modern Babylon— here is one view of what rooftop gardens can offer.

terraces, and rooftops. They are all small, urban gardens I have created over time. Depending on your own space, they can be replicated in whole or in part or simply used as a source of ideas to generate a garden of your own creation.

Although the focus of this book is the use of illusion to visually enlarge the small-space garden, it is equally important to ensure the best finished result in your design, regardless of garden size. The maxim "On Garden Design" (at the beginning of the book) simply describes how to achieve the design already inherent in the space and is explained later in greater detail.

Because this book is intended for the everyday gardener who gardens as a hobby for the sheer pleasure and relaxation it brings, I have chosen to use everyday terms and descriptions rather than technical jargon. For the same reason, I have also made extensive use of pictures for the extra visual clarity and ease of understanding they bring. In the case of plants, I have used the more familiar common names throughout the book; scientific nomenclature (mostly Latin) is kept to a minimum and only added to the common name where a specific species or cultivar is identified and recommended.

Few can question the rewards and pleasure of having a garden escape, however small. I hope that what follows will both stimulate your imagination and provide you the necessary design skills to get the maximum benefit and enjoyment from your small garden. If you achieve the feeling of satisfaction, tranquillity, and beauty that nature provides, this book has been worthwhile.

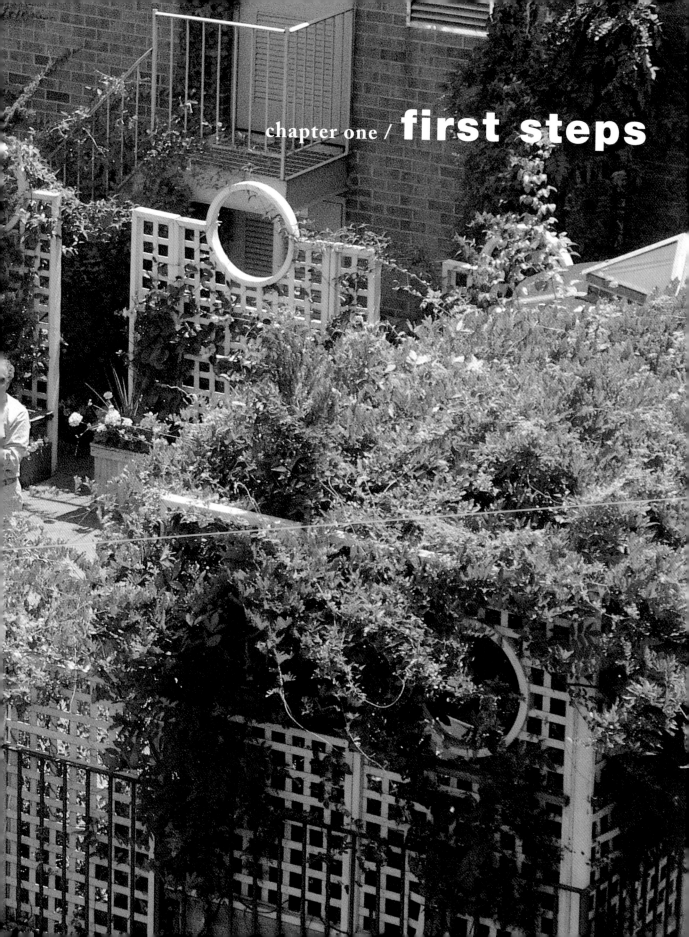

chapter one / **first steps**

know your space
before you start

creating a garden can seem quite daunting if it is something you have not attempted before. You are faced with a blank open space and a puzzle. Where do you begin? Designing a garden can be made easier and more manageable by following a logical sequence of steps to ensure as much as possible that you eventually end up with the best result.

The first step is to get to know your space before you begin to draw up a garden plan. This key step is sometimes overlooked or bypassed, but it is the most valuable one in that it sets the foundation for all that is to follow. This is especially true with a small-space garden because there is little room to maneuver due to the more tightly related elements. Getting to know the space before you begin drawing up a garden plan is of especially great value in a small garden because with good planning, you can make the space look larger than it really is.

The area can tell you a lot about itself. As you observe your space, you will begin to get a general sense of its physical reality—of its size and shape, its juxtaposition to the house and areas immediately adjacent to the perimeter, and the general area beyond. This gives an early indication of which features are

Fig. 1-1 (preceding page). Perched on even the smallest (34 by 28 feet) of rooftop spaces (and despite being hemmed in by the surrounding concrete jungle), a garden with a perimeter screen of lacy-leaved vines on a white trellis gives an outwardly flowing feeling. Even so, it still maintains plenty of living space within.

Fig. 1-2 (opposite). While "the mountain won't come to Muhammad," it can sometimes be made to appear to. In this case, the ocean appears to have come to and entered the garden, expanding the field of vision.

permanent, which lend themselves to modification, and which are removable. The value at this stage is that the space begins to provide clues about how the eventual garden may fit. For example, Fig. 1-2 shows a small seaside garden of only 20 by 30 feet. with its tidal pool, boulders, and grasses taking full advantage of the setting beyond to provide a good fit with the sea inlet. A well-designed garden blends with what you have and should flow from it. In this case, "borrowing" the vista helps overcome the feeling of smallness.

Conversely, an existing retaining wall topped with a high wire fence (Fig. 1-3) can screen out an unwanted view with attractive flowering vines and serve as a backdrop within the space itself. These are just two ways of turning existing conditions to your advantage; many others will be presented throughout this book.

Note in general terms other features, such as flow of the terrain, existing large trees, walls and buildings, and other dominant shapes. Even apparently featureless high rooftop spaces can offer clues to determining the theme or foundation of the garden that you can use later in preparing for the design process.

Relying on the eye and memory alone in this initial survey can be difficult, even for the most experienced garden designer. Our minds are easily distracted and, since the eye looks but does not always see, I have found that photographing the site is an excellent way to give a clearer and more objective overall sense of the possibilities and limitations. The camera records and captures everything more clearly and accurately. Photographing in black and white rather than color is particularly effective because it neutralizes the effect of the receding light colors (pastel

Fig. 1-3. Even elements in an existing garden can be retained and turned into positive features. Here, an unattractive wire mesh fence with clutter behind it is cloaked by a curtain of flowering vines.

shades) and the advancing bold, dark colors of certain features. In
color, these effects can distort the true prominence and size of the
items pictured.

When taking the pictures, stand in one spot and pivot
180 degrees, shooting overlapping frames as you go for complete
coverage of the space. Then tape the photographs together
sequentially so you can focus on the *whole area* as a single unit
rather than on many distracting details. You can more easily
identify the main lines—or "bones"—that will eventually form the
basis of the design and minimize the problem of not seeing the
forest for the trees.

A typical example of how this technique is applied is seen

in Fig. 1-4, showing a small 30-by-20-foot rundown space.
Although presented here in color rather than black and white,
the composite photograph tells immediately that the eventual
design will need to do three things. First, it must screen out the
somewhat derelict and wildly overgrown area that surrounds
the plot. Second, dominant elements of interest must be created
and built into the flat, featureless area inside the space. Third,
whatever plan we eventually arrive at for the garden, it should
have a welcome "oasis" feel of escape in contrast to the neighboring
environment.

At this stage, the design process involves determining
broadly what physically exists and needs to be done, but not how

**Fig. 1-4. Before you begin,
let the camera be your eyes,
seeing and reading more
accurately what you have.**

that will be achieved when it comes to the shape and structure of the plan.

Getting to know your space well also involves assessing growing conditions for the plants that will eventually fill the structure. Check for the hours of sunlight and shade, and whether your space is sheltered or exposed to the wind. A garden can look totally different from summer to winter—when the plants lose their color and leaves due to dormancy, as this snow-covered example (Fig. 1-5) of a rooftop garden demonstrates. A good time period for observation is six months to ensure you get a reliable read. Note also the extremes of heat and cold and consistency of rainfall. The climate zone map (page 142) will give you a good guide to plant hardiness for your geographical region.

A further good practice is to observe in a general way over the same period neighboring gardens that are similar to your own in condition and size and that are flourishing. Analyze the types of plant material that are used and see how well the design overcomes the problem of smallness. You don't have to be Sherlock Holmes. Once you know what to look for, the task is much easier.

Don't rush, and do ensure that you give your mind time to absorb all that you uncover. Allow your conscious and unconscious mind to flow naturally and freely as design ideas, broad shapes, plants, and possible solutions begin to emerge. These first steps will provide a foundation as you begin the design process with Chapter Four, "Developing the Design." And as you plan during the cold winter months, you will find the convenience of being able to study a composite photograph in the comfort of your warm home a decided advantage.

Fig. 1-5. Note the changes in your existing space between seasons. The snow-blanketed naked plants in winter give the garden a very different appearance from its summer look, seen in Fig. 1-1.

chapter two / **making your space seem larger**

smaller, yet still
a complete garden

by far, the biggest challenge in designing a small garden is overcoming the limited amount of space. Logic tells us that without the luxury of an acre or two, we have to forsake many of the interesting and fun features, such as a pond or gazebo, and limit considerably the greenery and flowers that are the essence of a garden. And gone would be the expansiveness where we could ramble and get lost in the seclusion of nature. So we are left with only a small outdoor space in which to garden and potter, yet we still desire and need the same satisfaction the owner of a more spacious garden has.

But with design techniques that involve the use of illusion to make the garden appear larger than it really is, it is possible to create a similar feeling in a smaller area.

Illusion is, of course, not something new. Artists have been using it ever since the 15th century, when Filippo Brunelleschi discovered the optical laws of linear perspective. Basically this enabled the painter to create a three-dimensional scene on a flat surface with the size of all the elements in direct proportion to one another as they recede to infinity. Being a painter as well as a

Fig. 2-1 (preceding page). Planting on the vertical plane can dramatically influence perception and create the illusion of a much larger garden. Here, perennial clematis and tropical mandevilla vines together provide a full splash of color throughout the whole summer season. The illusion is further supported by potted annual impatiens, geraniums, and begonias. At the back is a wall (partially seen at top) covered with spring-flowering wisteria, which adds more height to the illusion.

Fig. 2-2. The surprise of finding dwarf versions of exotic tropical palm trees (Phoenix *roebelenii* in planters for overwintering indoors) set among the temperate-climate plants is one of the more compelling methods of diverting the viewer's attention away from the size of the garden itself. Additionally, the scaled-down size and light, airy foliage add further to the feeling of greater spaciousness.

garden designer, I have been able to apply the principles of this law and recognize its value and relevance in creating the illusion necessary to overcome the limitations of small garden spaces.

Having always considered the garden an art form, it was a natural step for me to apply these principles, since the only creative difference is that the medium becomes the plants instead of paint. Both create a "canvas," even though one is living and ever-changing (plantscape) and the other is inert (oil paint). It is no accident that some of the best garden designers in recent history were also artists, such as Claude Monet, Gertrude Jekyll, and, more recently, Russell Page. The late Rosemary Verey, while not an actual painter, still brought the instincts of an artist's eye to all her garden creations. Her philosophy of considering the garden an art form was also widely known, and her designs were admired greatly.

So the garden designer can take a lesson from the artist by following the same disciplines and techniques: scale and proportion; depth and perspective; focus, balance, and composition; texture and tone; and color and tint. All are used to create illusion, whether it be a large landscape on a small canvas or a large garden on a small plot. If they look complete and right to the eye, we accept the illusion.

Even if you're not an artist, you may recognize these techniques. Some are used in interior design to make small rooms appear larger (reproportioned furniture and lighter, recessive colors, for example).

The following pages show how to apply these techniques to your small garden space. Nine main design techniques can be used to make the small garden space look bigger. They are illustrated on pages 32–33. A discussion of them completes this

Fig. 2-3. Scale and proportion can help overcome the limitations of even the narrowest of garden spaces.

chapter. They all have the effect of controlling the eye when viewing the garden to give the illusion of greater space.

1. Scale and Proportion

Of the nine illusion techniques mentioned, scale and proportion are the most important and essential when designing a small garden. While the other techniques are optional and interchangeable according to site conditions, it is not possible to achieve the feeling of a full and complete garden unless every item is scaled down proportionately to fit the limited space. This applies to everything from plants to structures to paved areas. The idea is to retain as many elements as possible that are associated with a larger space and that you desire for your own enjoyment and satisfaction. A useful analogy is that of a model railroad train or dollhouse: All the elements of a full-size railroad or house are present in a complete and harmonious manner—they're just smaller.

Obviously, there are limits on how much can be included, since urban spaces are notoriously small, but the discipline of scale and proportion can still work effectively. For example, the very narrow high-terraced garden in Fig. 2-3 (page 29), while 25 feet long, is only 40 inches wide. In order to achieve the effect presented, everything was carefully scaled down. To allow access, the planters take up just one-third of the width of the space. They are planted with dwarf or small, slow-growing conifers (spruce and juniper), and low-growing perennials (daylily) and annuals (impatiens, begonia, and vertical standards of marguerite) to maintain the proportions and avoid the garden design becoming overgrown with the passage of time. The only exception to slow growth is the use of vines (clematis) and climbers (roses) for their

yearly surge of vertical and overhead growth to cover the metal
tubular arches. Vines and climbers provide disproportionate
fullness of foliage and flowers relative to the planter/floor space
they occupy.

2. Using All Three Planes

Using all three planes (vertical, overhead, and the ground) to carry
foliage and flowers is the second-most-important design technique
for overcoming the lack of floor space in every small garden. Using
all three planes can increase the growing area threefold or more
compared with conventional ground-plane planting alone and
avoids the feeling of overcrowding. The terrace space in Fig. 2-4,
only 10 feet wide, shows how the use of an overhead arbor and
wall-mounted trellis provides the support for climbing wisteria

Fig. 2-4. Using all three
planes means more garden
and the chance to be
immersed in nature.

Summary of Design Techniques
to Counter Smallness

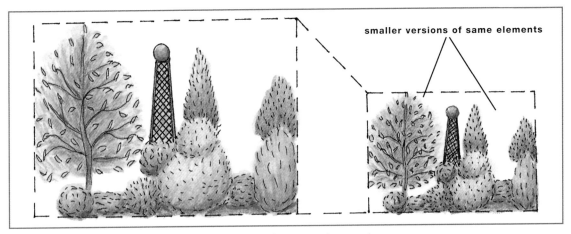

1. Scale and Proportion. Reduce everything for a complete garden.

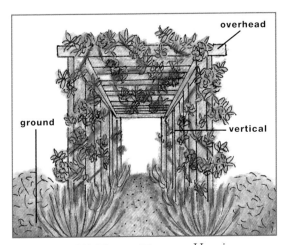

2. Using All Three Planes. Here is a space-efficient choice that makes room for more foliage

3. Expanding Beyond the Perimeter. Extend the line of vision so there's more to see.

4. Different Levels and Sections. Divert interest from the size of the garden.

5. Providing a Focal Point. Draw the eye into the garden.

6. Using Circles and Curves. Slow down the viewer's eye.

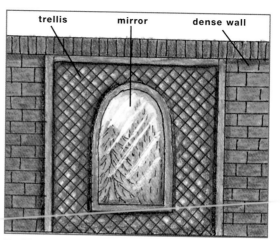

7. Neutralizing Encroachments. Minimize the impact of unattractive, solid areas.

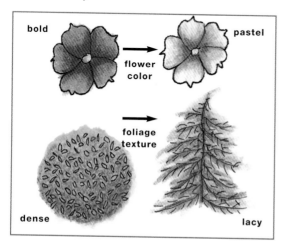

8. Lighter Texture and Color. Use these techniques for openness and spaciousness.

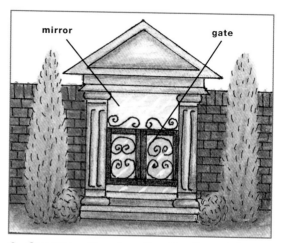

9. Creating Greater Depth. Extend the garden outside and beyond your space.

and clematis, while still leaving open space in the center. The design is supported on the left by vertical-growing plants (cherry tree and perennial daisies), which provide a pleasing balance and composition. Being surrounded by plants in this manner helps enhance the feeling and illusion of escape in the garden and is the result of fully utilizing all three planes.

3. Expanding Beyond the Perimeter

While of course physically we can't plant outside the boundaries of our small space, certain techniques direct or encourage the eye outward from within the garden. The effect is to open the range of vision by blending the garden with what lies beyond and thereby counteract the cramped, claustrophobic feel of a confined small space. This may be likened to the difference between being in a glass solarium or a totally enclosed room of the same size.

There are two main ways of advancing beyond the perimeter. The first (Fig. 2-5) is blending or creating a good fit, where this townhouse rooftop garden is positioned against and under a hundred-year-old London plane tree growing from below for an uninterrupted flow of greenery. So, while this small space of only 20 by 20 feet gains the collateral benefit of dappled shade, it achieves the overall feeling of expansiveness both above and beyond.

The second way "borrows the vista" by framing the view beyond, as in Fig. 2-6. Although it uses the same techniques of expanding beyond the perimeter, it relies more on utilizing the artist's way of creating depth and perspective. This terrace is only 4 feet wide by 6 feet long, requiring us to go look elsewhere to create interest. Though there is barely enough room for a few small planters and a single chair, the garden captures the adjacent

Fig. 2-5 (opposite, top). Blending in and flowing from the immediate environment add greater expansiveness.

Fig. 2-6 (opposite, bottom). Why not borrow the dramatic panorama beyond if it adds depth and perspective to your tiny space?

park below and the far high-rises beyond, framing them with clematis vines and alstromeria. "Borrowed" it may be, but it gives the focused eye a panoramic spread that even the largest of gardens would be happy to match.

4. Different Levels and Sections

We are often struck by how small a flat urban garden can be. This is usually because nothing detracts the eye from taking in the whole space with one glance. Creating different levels and sections helps change this perception by directing the eye toward specific parts of the garden that hold the viewer's interest.

Fig. 2-7 is a view of the *inside* of the rooftop garden shown in Fig. 2-5, which uses multilevel decking as well as raised and sunken planters rising up to a high-stepped seating area. These combine to create interest and awareness within the small garden space. By way of comparison, consider a flat, featureless plane and a space of equal size with mountains, hills, and dales. In the former, all there is to see is size; in the latter, the interesting terrain makes the size secondary.

5. Providing a Focal Point

Providing a focal point capitalizes on the natural tendency to seek out one item of interest at a time. We are psychologically more comfortable focusing than floating without a sense of direction. When we first see the area, we're drawn to one particular item rather than the garden as a whole, and we overlook its smallness. The focal point can be a statue, pond, obelisk, gazebo, or even a pleasingly shaped large rock. It can be almost anything, provided it fits well with the overall style of the garden.

For example, the seating area in Fig. 2-8—with its cast-iron bench flanked with finials deliberately painted a highly visible pastel blue—immediately captures one's attention on entry into this small, 18-by-25-foot backyard garden. The bench beckons with a restful and tempting invitation, overriding any thoughts about garden size.

Controlling the eye in this manner is a little like being in a maze: The attention required to make all the many twists and turns to reach the center successfully shifts the focus from the smallness of the maze.

Fig. 2-7. Variations in level and section heighten the interest within the garden, diminishing awareness of and concern about its size.

6. Using Circles and Curves

Circles and curves slow down the eye and eliminate the natural
tendency to speed up that occurs with straight lines. Because they
are appealing and pleasurable, circles and curves capture attention
and direct it away from the overall structure and size of the garden
to individual features within it. Curves predominate in nature;
straight lines suggest the overdeveloped, unnatural working world.
Compare the monotony of a boring superhighway, for example,
with the pleasure of a meandering country lane that sustains our
interest and attention.

The garden in Fig. 2-9 sits in a backyard only 30 feet long
by 24 feet wide; its small size is eclipsed by flower beds of various
shapes set in the lawn. Each curve holds the promise of more to
come and gives the feeling of a parklike atmosphere, as we amble
along in the garden.

**Fig. 2-8 (opposite). Draw in
the eye with an inviting lure
to shift the focus away from
the smallness of the garden.**

**Fig. 2-9 (above). Slow
down with leisurely curves
and circles—they appear
frequently in nature.**

7. Neutralizing Encroachments

In one way or another, walls are usually a part of most small urban gardens—and sometimes loom disproportionately larger than the growing area itself. They can be the actual wall of the house, a separate wall delineating the house, or a very high wall for privacy. In all cases, their mass imposes itself and visually "advances" into the garden, further reinforcing the feeling of smallness.

The solution is to use a light-colored texture to neutralize the encroachment. This helps avoid the visual loss of space and accompanying claustrophobic feeling. The texture of a wall-mounted trellis, a whitewashed wall, or the lacy leaves of climbing ivy all work well to achieve this. They can be used individually or in concert, as shown on this high wall at the back of the garden in Fig. 2-10. Here, a mirror-backed Palladian window–styled trellis combines with quick-growing Boston ivy and the high vertical evergreen canes of bamboo to make the wall vanish almost completely throughout the winter and summer.

8. Lighter Texture and Color

Lighter leaf texture and flower color bring a sense of openness and spaciousness to the heart of the garden itself. This technique is based on the fact that bold colors and shapes advance, whereas lighter ones recede to give a more open and airy feel—an ethereal, atmospheric quality. Lightness and texture, or fading, are the characteristics the eye associates with distance; as things get farther away, the smaller and less distinct they become. Transposing these qualities (the artist's "depth and perspective") to benefit the small garden creates the illusion of considerably greater size.

Despite the closeness of the planting, the garden in Fig. 2-11 is still able to retain the feeling of openness by combining the laciness of weeping birch, the featheriness of spreading Japanese maple, and the underplanting of impatiens—all of which are light in color and texture.

9. Creating Greater Depth

Creating the illusion of greater depth is a way of visually expanding beyond the back portion of the perimeter to give the impression that the garden extends twice the length it really does. Various methods are often mentioned for achieving this effect, but many fall short—either because they don't look right to the eye or because they look contrived. They fail to capture the feeling of depth in a convincing manner.

One such approach is to decrease the actual size of the trees and shrubs from front to back. The problem is, this creates exactly the opposite effect when looking toward the front of the garden from the back—the trees and shrubs then become larger the farther away they are.

The technique of continuously reducing or distorting the width of the flower beds or paths from front to back creates a similar problem. Even trompe l'oeil (from the 17th-century French formal garden style)—using distorted converging trellis laths to create depth perception—falls flat, because using lines alone is far too abstract and lacks realism. As a result, it becomes merely decorative.

The use of mirrors, on the other hand, not only avoids these problems, but in terms of sheer illusion is by far the best method for extending depth. For example, the partial scene at the end of a 20-by-20-foot backyard garden (Fig. 2-12) uses a

Fig. 2-10 (above). Push back an imposing wall to avoid making the space look smaller than it really is.

Fig. 2-11 (opposite). Light texture and color contribute significantly to the feeling of a much larger space.

combination of items, among them a mirror-enclosed brick and a gated doorway. This is reinforced by built-up brick beds and steps rising to the entry gate. Not only does this project the style and the garden plants into the illusionary space beyond to give greater matching; but it gives a technically believable appearance—the lines continuing the depth perspective are most convincing to the eye.

What better than the realism of the mirror image itself to achieve the objective? Put another way, while an abstract cubist portrait by Picasso may be impressive, the realism of Gainsborough achieves true recognition and acceptance.

Technique Application and Usage

With the exception of reduced scale and proportion, which is essential to all small gardens, the use of other illusion techniques is largely determined by the needs of your own particular space and the opportunities it may present. The ideal, of course, is to use as many as possible—adapted or modified to suit the style of garden—to gain the maximum overall effect.

Bear in mind that individual techniques are described only by their main attribute for clarity, and some overlapping and combining does occur. So it is not essential to keep each technique distinct and separate. For example, the mirror in Fig.2-12 that demonstrates "greater depth" also portrays "point of focus" and "different levels and sections" for additional visual support. This is equally true in many other examples throughout this book.

Fig. 2-12 (opposite). A mirrored false entry point gives the impression that the garden continues beyond the door. Note the absence of the photographer's image in the mirror. This is ingeniously achieved by slightly angling outward two vertically abutting half mirrors; this technique further contributes to the illusion of greater depth.

from patio to penthouse
and places in between

provide moisture, nutrients, quality light, a place for roots to anchor and grow, and a garden can be created in almost any urban space, regardless of shape, form, location, or size. It can be an enclosed and sheltered backyard or an exposed high-rise rooftop. It can be an expansive penthouse with a magnificent vista, the merest sliver of a balcony or a spacious wraparound terrace. It can even be a cramped courtyard hemmed in by neighboring buildings.

Because of this wide variety in the types of urban garden space, the way in which illusion techniques can be applied will vary according to the type and characteristics of the space. For example, if there are no attractive views, you would not select the technique of visually expanding the vista; likewise you wouldn't choose an arbor on a small balcony. Chapter Six, "Garden Structures," will address the selection, placement, and construction of elements in greater depth.

For now we will discuss individual types of garden space, to give you a basic idea of the main characteristics of and differences among each. It will help in identifying your own space and will cover the possibilities for using the design illusion techniques.

Fig. 3-1 (preceding page). Trellises are versatile and offer endless decorative design possibilities to screen out an oppressively high back wall. While visually helping to enlarge a small garden space, here the peacock design also helps draw the focus to the central fountain.

Fig. 3-2 (opposite). Curved perennial flowerbeds intersected with paved paths provide a flowing motion and define separate areas in the garden to hold interest.

Backyard

The urban backyard garden space is probably the type we are most familiar with. It ranges in size from one-twentieth of an acre (2,178 square feet) to about one-tenth of an acre (4,356 square feet), and can even be as small as one-fiftieth of an acre (871 square feet). The typical backyard is either oblong or square and is enclosed with a fence, hedge, or high wall for privacy from neighboring houses and gardens. Privacy—although sometimes illusory, as neighboring buildings continue to soar—is a luxury to be cherished in a crowded urban environment. While surrounding buildings may limit the amount of sunlight hours, the backyard garden may also benefit from the moderating effect of the ground—a plus that balcony, terrace, and penthouse gardens high up lose.

Depending on your garden style preference and needs, the backyard offers the best opportunity to use space-illusion techniques to visually expand the space. As the finished example on page 79 shows, a full range of small plants is possible, with many different hardscape features and design options—all normally associated only with larger gardens. And the backyard garden is also far less difficult to create and install than, say, a rooftop garden, because fewer bureaucratic restrictions cramp your style. Additionally, the logistics of material delivery are easier at ground level.

The photos in Figs. 3-2, 3-3, and 3-4 show the backyard of a school for underprivileged children in a rundown neighborhood. The objective was twofold: to create a quiet, restful retreat from the turmoil outside and to expose the children to the beauty of nature—both of which they would otherwise have little chance to experience. While the space is only 40 feet long by 60 feet wide,

the technique of reduced scale and proportion creates a sense of spaciousness and an open, peaceful, parklike atmosphere. This is made even more effective by screening out the rest of the world with a surrounding flowering vine-covered fence. Scaling also gave the chance to include such hardscape items as benches, an arbor, an outdoor chessboard, paved walkways, and a fountain. The trunks of the inherited tall ailanthus trees can be seen reaching beyond the top of Fig. 3-3, and they were incorporated into the design to give vertical height and dappled shade. Their large, gnarled shape also gave the garden a sense of maturity and character, qualities often missing in a new garden.

The curved annual and perennial flower beds have been raised with bricks and edged in bluestone pavers for definition and are set in the lawn in a way that gives a great sense of anticipation around each curve and a flowing movement throughout the whole garden. Using the illusion technique of curves captures and diverts the attention away from the small size of the area.

Fig. 3-3 (above, left). A surrounding vine-covered hedge ensures privacy and a mood of quiet seclusion from the hustle and bustle outside. The upward thrust of the tall trunks of existing trees gives a feeling of spaciousness.

Fig. 3-4 (above, right). Paved edging provides greater definition for the flowerbeds of varying shapes.

Interestingly enough, the basic design is based on the shapes of an old upright piano harp found in the backyard (Fig. 3-5), a reminder that serendipity plays an important role in the creative process and has resulted in some of the finest ideas and inventions.

Patio

As a living space immediately adjacent to the house, the patio is usually very small and fully paved over for living use, leaving little ground, if any, for planting. Therefore, patios often rely on brick planters or cutout beds around the perimeter to minimize encroachment on the already limited central area. The main design requirement for this kind of space is to visually push back the perimeter and create a vertical accent to compensate, focusing more on hardscape features than plantings.

Fig. 3-5 (above). The gold-plated piano harp makes an excellent piece of sculpture and forms the basis for this garden design.

Fig. 3-6 (opposite, top). Capturing and creating the maximum light possible is essential for this small semi-shaded patio.

Fig. 3-7 (opposite, bottom). The mirrors on the door shown reflect the view from ones in a facing door.

The patio garden photographed in Figs. 3-6 and 3-7 is only 18 feet wide by 18 feet long but is surrounded by an 8-foot-high white trellis with framed doorway-size mirrors at either end. The two features combine to open up the space as the white of the trellis recedes, while the mirrors reflect not only the garden but each other repeatedly to infinity for a feeling of depth and perspective. The small waterfall at the left end of the garden stirs the sense of sound with its splashing motion and evokes feelings of tranquillity—a quality most desired in an urban setting.

The light, airy foliage texture of shade-tolerant bamboo underplanted with ferns (which requires only two hours of direct sunlight a day) reinforces the feeling of spaciousness.

The overall effect of lightness is clearly evident in Fig 3-6, the overhead picture of the garden; contrast it with the gloom of the neighboring empty space to its right.

Fig. 3-8. The light colors
of blue plumbago, pink
bougainvillea, and white
chrysanthemum combine
to make a summer-only
garden.

Balcony

The balcony, perhaps the smallest of urban spaces in which to create a garden, requires a rather different treatment from most other types of space. Not only is the size itself very limiting, but one must also consider how much weight it can hold as an overhang from the building. Additionally, its height off the ground leaves it exposed to the winter elements; it lacks the moderating benefits of an in-ground garden. Furthermore, there is no room for hardscape items (except for perhaps a small piece of trellis for climbers), leaving total reliance on plants for the design. All plants should be treated as annuals and planted in lightweight plastic pots for summer enjoyment only, since balcony conditions can be too harsh for even the hardiest of perennials to overwinter.

With barely enough room for one chair, the 5-by-6-foot balcony in Figs. 3-8 and 3-9, uses a light palette of silver, white, and sky blue with just a touch of pink to counter the size with the feeling of airiness. To keep the garden at its peak as the season progresses and the flowers fade, the plants can be changed easily with later-blooming ones.

One asset of a small space is that even the most inexperienced gardener can create a little oasis during the warmer months when the balcony is in use.

Fig. 3-9. There is room at least for a chair, to sit amongst summer flowers, even on the smallest of balconies.

Rooftop

A rooftop space offers excellent potential for creating a garden in an urban environment. The area available, whether on a townhouse or a tall apartment building, is often larger than the typical backyard and offers potential for the widest range of space illusion techniques. By far the greatest advantage of being high off the ground is the vista that surrounds the space, which gives a built-in sense of openness, allowing the eye to travel well beyond the perimeter of the garden itself. Very often the views are more interesting and dramatic than those offered in a more spacious and open rural garden.

However, the design potential notwithstanding, in practical terms building a rooftop garden presents an entirely different set of conditions than at ground level. The most obvious is that there

Fig. 3-10. A rooftop garden offers a chance to bask in the cool breezes on high at the end of a summer's day, as the sun drops behind the still-steamy, crowded urban panorama below.

are no natural elements for growing things, so all the materials (soil, planters, plants, etc.) must be brought up from ground level. Climate and plant-care considerations also come into play, as will be seen in later chapters.

The rooftop garden in Figs. 3-10 and 3-11 is on top of a 38-story apartment building. The design takes full advantage of the imposing vista by allowing the eye to travel beyond the perimeter to give the illusion of spaciousness to this 30-by-40-foot area. The viewer can bask in a large, hardy evergreen garden at the sides and back, but because the front has been left low, the whole focus is taken far beyond the perimeter. It becomes a little like a Roman amphitheater: The distant view becomes the stage and player; the garden itself, the viewing platform.

Fig 3-11. Upright evergreen conifers echo the high vertical building towers in the background.

Courtyard

The courtyard is usually the most secluded of all garden spaces because it is surrounded by walls on all four sides. Although larger than a patio, the space is still very small. Scale and proportion are better limited by reducing plant size in the central part of the garden than by adding hardscape structures; an approach that will maintain the openness of the space. However, climbing vines on perimeter wall–mounted trellises add additional foliage to the vertical plane, giving a feeling of a fuller garden.

In the case of the 20-by-30-foot inner courtyard in Figs. 3-12 and 3-13, the unusual decision was made to move the viewing vantage point from within the garden to the perimeter of the living space inside instead. The fact that the garden is highly visible through floor-to-ceiling glass windows from almost every angle created more room for plants within. Using the space in this way allows for a fuller, more complete garden. The garden itself becomes the focal point, rather than a single point of interest within the garden. And although this is counter to the usual technique of detracting the eye from the smallness of the space, the rare opportunity provided by the glass wall allows the same architectural style for both the inside and outside. Together they blend and flow uninterrupted, further enhancing the illusion of a larger space. By adding small plants with an airy texture, a feeling of great space is achieved.

Fig. 3-12 (opposite). A wrap-around living space makes the whole garden the focal point for viewing, rather than one spot within the garden being the main point.

Fig. 3-13 (above). The clean architectural lines of the deck and planters match those within the house itself.

Terrace

Urban living continues to rise higher and becomes more crowded as buildings get taller, so the terrace has become the most common space after the backyard for creating a garden. Some terraces are only a few floors up from the ground, while others are many stories high. In these gardens, pots and containers are the sole method of planting.

Although mostly long and narrow, terraces still lend themselves well to creating the feeling of a full and complete garden. Scaling everything down in size and using foliage on all three planes are the two main illusion techniques to apply in terrace gardening. Adding vine-covered arches or arbors is another effective technique, breaking the space into sections and helping to divert attention from the smallness of the overall space.

If the trees and shrubs chosen are small and medium types, and if they are slow-growing and suited to the confines of planters, then a wide variety of plant choices is available for the garden. Because terraces tend to be lower than most rooftops and less shaded than confined ground-level gardens, you can choose less hardy, more sun-loving plants.

Although narrow width is a dominant design consideration for hardscape items, this need not limit the imagination in terms of amount and type. Arbors, trellises, decking, built-in benches, fountains, and other elements can still be used by making the fit narrower than normal. That is an important design element in creating the illusion of larger space—the fewer the items of interest, the greater the awareness of space limitations.

As with any aboveground garden on a building, equal emphasis should be given to construction considerations as to style when developing the plan, remembering that buildings were not built with gardens in mind.

While only the main south-facing section of the U-shaped wraparound terrace is shown in Fig. 3-14, the two remaining legs continue in the same pattern. Its built-in turns are a decidedly good advantage in that they naturally prevent seeing the whole garden in one glance. This is a key design technique for distracting the eye from the smallness of the space. Each turn is flanked by quarter radial arbors, which cover the main seating areas. The arbors not only break up the monotony of the long, narrow space (60 feet long by 8 feet wide), but they also serve to attract and lure the eye by holding the promise of more garden to come. Curiosity is one of the strongest motivators in human nature and should be utilized whenever possible in a small garden.

This terrace has no attractive outside views or vistas to rely on for the illusion of greater spaciousness, so all the interest has to come from the garden itself. Perimeter planting with a vertical "wall" of vines, long and narrow evergreens, and espaliered shrubs in narrow planters not only provide screened privacy but reinforce the line of vision and interest inside. Interior interest is further sustained with a wide mix of plant types whose range is associated with large gardens: Impatiens, salvia, climbing roses, wisteria, birch, juniper, and spruce can be seen in Fig. 3-14; cleome, hibiscus, yarrow, clematis, and pine are visible in Fig. 3-15.

Fig. 3-14 (opposite). Careful
scaling down of both the
hardscape and plants allows
the fullest of gardens in even
the narrowest of spaces.

Fig. 3-15 (above). A good
mix of plants is pleasurable
and heightens interest in
the garden.

Penthouse

The mere mention of a penthouse immediately conjures up visions of grandeur, spaciousness, and exciting vistas. Embellish it with a garden, and you have all the ingredients to create an urban retreat.

A penthouse gives the designer a head start. The design techniques to minimize smallness already exist in part and need only be identified and built on; the designer is not faced with the usual blank canvas. With the foundation having been laid by the architecture of the building, the style of the hardscape items should flow from this and blend for a good fit. In the relative spaciousness of a penthouse, creating the illusion of space through scale and proportion can be amplified to give an even greater feeling of a full and complete garden. Like the commanding view

Fig. 3-16. Low front planting emphasizes the magnificent vista beyond and keeps it open.

of an aerie, the vista beyond the garden becomes the focal point, creating the ambiance of unlimited expansiveness within the garden itself.

As with any other aboveground garden that sits on a building, the logistics involved in bringing everything up piecemeal continue to apply, as do practicing sound installation practices and observing regulations.

In the duplex penthouse garden in Fig. 3-16, the main design emphasis is to leave an unbroken panoramic vista of the city. This is accomplished by placing small plants all around the front perimeter and gradually increasing their height toward the back. As the plants climb higher, they make full use of the vertical plane, giving a feeling of a fuller garden as the foliage unifies the two levels (Fig. 3-17), which together measure 1,200 square feet.

Planted mainly with medium-to-small slow-growing hardy evergreens to withstand the harsh winter exposure, the lower main garden with its winter conservatory and summer arbor on the left has cozy vantage points for all seasons.

There is little awareness of a small-space garden here, as it sits high above the madding crowd.

Fig. 3-17. Vertical vines cover the walls to unite the two levels.

chapter four / **developing the design**

the need to plan
before you plant

a word on design I have found that the best approach in planning a small garden (or any size garden, for that matter), is to let the space and other existing factors tell you what the design should be. Taking this approach makes the design process both more logical and easier to follow and results in the best kind of garden, an idea summed up by the maxim that appears at the front of the book.

This philosophy ensures that the design flows from the external architectural style of the house, blends in with the natural setting and location of elements immediately surrounding the garden plot, and reflects the owner's passions, personality, and lifestyle. In short, the design should be the right fit for the right place.

Have you ever visited a garden and, although some things were quite stunning and others beautiful, it just didn't feel quite right, though you weren't sure why? For example, a Japanese garden would be out of place with the architecture of a colonial house; a natural garden would look quite odd with the interior décor of a neat and orderly person; a modern-style garden would conflict with the old-fashioned charm and rustic feel of a Greenwich Village–type setting.

Fig. 4-1 (preceding page). An arbor is always a welcome addition to any small garden. Because it can carry more foliage and flowers on both the vertical and overhead planes, it enhances the feeling of a larger garden. Here, coverage is provided by wisteria vine and climbing roses. These are a welcome treat for both rest and shade—and also for the privacy they offer from other closely abutting buildings that are a reality in a tight urban setting.

Figure 4-2 (opposite). Stroll down a country lane high above the city? Well, not literally, but good planning and an imaginative fit in this narrow space make it feel possible.

Do not be too ready to impose a given style of garden on your space at the initial stage of the design process. This is especially key for the urban gardener, where the overriding priority is to enlarge the plot visually for maximum satisfaction and to create the feeling of a fuller and more complete garden. With that objective in mind, personal style preferences, compatibility, and good fit will evolve naturally and logically as the design progresses.

The following steps will help guide and discipline you as you set about developing the plan for your own individual space.

(*Note:* Although the backyard garden is the most common type and is used to demonstrate the procedure, the same method is applicable to *all* types of small gardens.)

Step 1: Existing Space

After going through the initial process of becoming familiar with your space as outlined in Chapter One, "First Steps," you will already begin forming ideas about what is practical and what you would like in your new garden. By all means, make a note of them, but hold off on applying them until you determine what you already have.

As you begin the design process on paper (see Fig. 4-3), it is most important to draw everything carefully to scale. Using graph paper (where, for example, one square equals one foot) makes it simple and ensures a high degree of accuracy.

The first step is to measure the perimeter of your space and draw it on the grid. Then, using the sample backyard garden as a guide, write in everything that currently exists, giving all the dimensions. Include entryways, delivery access, windows, walls,

Fig. 4-3. Step 1.

Observations and conclusions
Utilize existing ground depressions to develop three different levels and break the garden into three sections. Remove all existing trees to allow full sunlight into all parts of the garden. Take advantage of the vista at the southwest corner, and use it for viewing the sunset. Screen out unwanted views at the eastern and southern portions of the perimeter. Soften or neutralize imposing side walls and the back of the house. Eliminate the path to allow freedom in developing a new design. Remove all smaller shrubs and trees. Make provisions for drainage. The southern exposure offers excellent growing conditions for the widest possible range of plants.

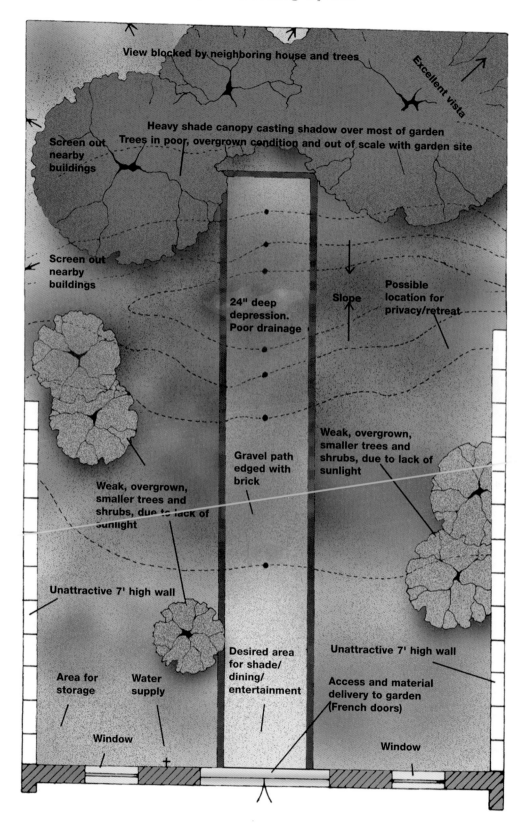

View blocked by neighboring house and trees

Excellent vista

S

Heavy shade canopy casting shadow over most of garden
Trees in poor, overgrown condition and out of scale with garden site

Screen out nearby buildings

Screen out nearby buildings

24" deep depression. Poor drainage

Slope

Possible location for privacy/retreat

Weak, overgrown, smaller trees and shrubs, due to lack of sunlight

Gravel path edged with brick

Weak, overgrown, smaller trees and shrubs, due to lack of sunlight

Unattractive 7' high wall

Unattractive 7' high wall

Desired area for shade/ dining/ entertainment

Access and material delivery to garden (French doors)

Area for storage

Water supply

Window

Window

pitch of ground, drainage outlets, and outside faucets. Indicate attractive areas, such as vistas, and any unsightly items—walls or chimneys or neighborhood buildings, for example—you may wish to screen out or hide. A large tree could be robbing your space of light and nutrients, not to mention being totally out of proportion to the size of the space. Hours of sunlight and partial shade should be noted, as well as the degree of exposure to the elements, since this will eventually determine plant selection.

Be sure to list your observations and conclusions on your drawing plan. These findings will form the basis for all that follows. For example, in the sample, the comments basically indicate that most of the conditions need to be changed and indicate the direction of the developing new design. The comments identify opportunities to exploit as well as problems to correct or eliminate.

Step 2: The Hardscape

Having analyzed the existing space and identified problem areas and some initial opportunities, the next step in creating the garden plan is developing the hardscape. The hardscape forms the structural framework, or "bones" of the garden, and consists of all the items made of inert materials (wood, stone, brick, slate, cement, plastic, metal, glass, etc.) that may be used for building the garden—in other words, everything except the plants (see Fig. 4-4a.).

Continue using the same scale on graph paper as on the sample, using tracing paper over the Step 1 drawing. This serves as a continuous reminder of both what you have and what the proper scale is that must be maintained accurately and constantly as you add the elements of the new design. It also saves much time and work, by avoiding repetition of perimeter lines and other fixed objects (windows, doors, etc.) in each step of the design process.

The drawing in the Step 2 example (Fig. 4-4b) takes full advantage of all the design illusion techniques covered in Chapter Two. How, where, and why are explained in the caption accompanying the drawing. For a good fit and flow, the garden structures you choose will take into account both your personal style and a sense of what will complement the existing architecture. (A wide range of hardscape examples is pictured in Chapter Six, "Garden Structures.")

Begin by penciling in on the tracing-paper overlay the largest or most important feature of the design. Follow that with the other items in descending order of size and priority. In this example, three separate areas and levels are created to form the main foundation of the design. They follow the natural terrain of the ground. As well as achieving the main objective of stopping the eye from taking in the whole garden at a glance (as it would the existing garden), this creates two other important benefits. First, the "main garden," in taking up almost half the space, conveys a sense of openness immediately upon entering, and has enough space for the most-used functional area. Second, the "lower" and "higher" levels gradually decrease in size both visually and physically, adding to the feeling of greater depth.

The next step is to draw in the path to link the three areas together. In unifying the whole garden this way, note how a curved, meandering path is used, rather than a straight line, to slow the eye down. The curved path is at least twice as long and provides a more leisurely lure of things to come—another

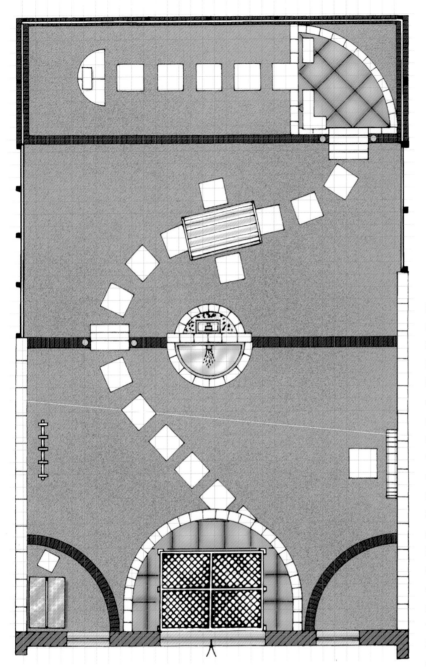

1 square = 1 foot

Fig. 4-4. Step 2.

Design illusion techniques

Note the use of three different levels, breaking the space into separate gardens. Note also the use of curves (edging and paths, etc.) and focal points (fountain, arch, and vista); the provision for vertical and overhead flowers and foliage; and the traditional ground plane. Linking all three gardens with the paved paths helps provide flow. The use of light, airy trellis sructures and the creation of a vista platform all visually open up the perimeter. And finally, all hardscape items have been scaled down in proportion to each other and to the size of the space. Altogether these techniques help overcome the smallness of the space and give the feeling and illusion of a larger and complete garden.

Step 2: The Hardscape

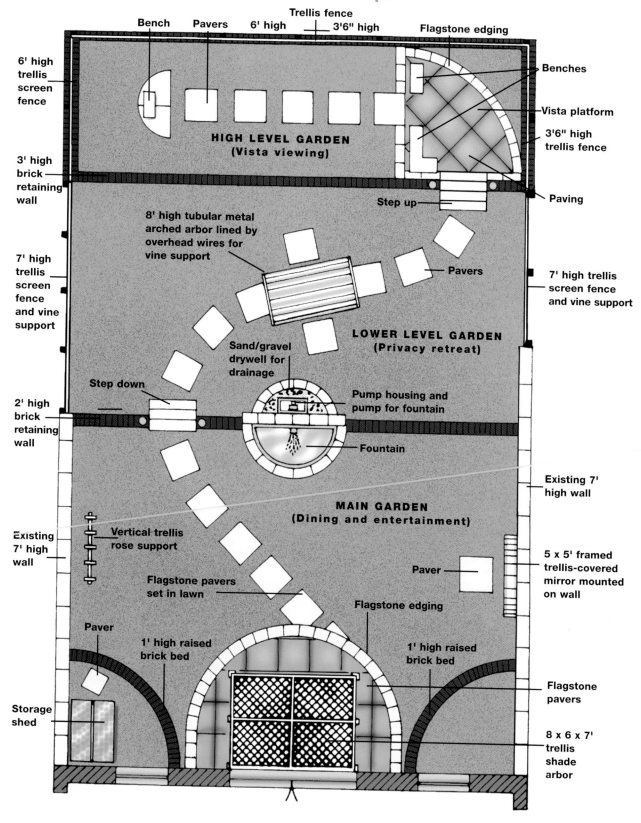

Bench **Pavers** **6' high** **Trellis fence** **3'6" high** **Flagstone edging**

6' high trellis screen fence

3' high brick retaining wall

7' high trellis screen fence and vine support

2' high brick retaining wall

Existing 7' high wall

Storage shed

Paver

HIGH LEVEL GARDEN (Vista viewing)

Benches

Vista platform

3'6" high trellis fence

Paving

Step up

8' high tubular metal arched arbor lined by overhead wires for vine support

Pavers

7' high trellis screen fence and vine support

LOWER LEVEL GARDEN (Privacy retreat)

Sand/gravel drywell for drainage

Pump housing and pump for fountain

Step down

Fountain

MAIN GARDEN (Dining and entertainment)

Existing 7' high wall

5 x 5' framed trellis-covered mirror mounted on wall

Vertical trellis rose support

Paver

Flagstone pavers set in lawn

Flagstone edging

1' high raised brick bed

1' high raised brick bed

Flagstone pavers

8 x 6 x 7' trellis shade arbor

characteristic normally associated with much larger gardens. Note also that each section has its own focal point, the fountain in the main garden, where the sight and sound of the water can best be enjoyed, the arch in the lower-level garden, which is such fun to pass through, and the distant vista from the highest-level garden.

The shade arbor and paved dining area underneath are then added to the plan, with sufficient room for furniture. In determining the style to follow for continuity and fit, arbors—because of their size and visibility—are usually the best places to incorporate key architectural features of a house. Note the continuing use of curves as the paved patio and raised brick beds are positioned. Note how they are repeated later in the design of the foundation and vista platform to add flow and movement to the garden. The remaining items such as fences, dry well, benches, rose support, wall mirror, etc., are then finally added to complete the hardscape design.

Now is the time to step back and review the plan to ensure that nothing has been overlooked. It is almost certain that some fine-tuning will be needed at this stage for a well-balanced and pleasing design to result. Check for the following: First and foremost, make sure the size of all elements is directly proportional to one other and the overall space, otherwise the illusion of a larger garden will be compromised. Next, check the accuracy of the size of the individual items; avoid the temptation to fudge a little for the sake of a more pleasing design on paper. Remember that what you do now will eventually become the working guide or shop drawing for the garden. Also, make sure you do not over-fill the design. Overcrowding can create the opposite effect of openness—besides leaving too little room for plants.

Finally, remind yourself that hardscape is the bone structure of a garden. No amount of cosmetic cover-up (in this case, the plants) can ever really correct deficiencies or create the level of quality and beauty good structure permanently confers.

Step 3: The Plantscape and Finished Design

The plantscape, or plant material, is all the living and growing matter that when laid into the design, completes the finished plan on paper. The plantscape is fundamental to why we garden, provides the crowning glory to all that is done with hardscape, and brings the garden to life.

Unlike hardscape items (which can be tailored exactly), the key to using plants in designing is understanding that from the myriad types available, very few actually qualify for the task, and we have to find them. So the main consideration is the selection process—choosing from a range of plants what will work best to create an illusion that the garden is larger than it really is. The main illusion techniques are small trees and shrubs, plants with vertical and overhead growth, and plants that are light in color and texture. Most gardeners have their plant favorites, and growing conditions vary by individual site. Don't even think about that until you're sure a plant meets the basic requirement of making the garden appear larger. As a further guide, refer to the plant overview in Chapter Seven and the extensive plant list in the Appendix.

As you begin positioning your plants, use a tracing-paper overlay, as before (see Fig. 4-5b). This will help you tie in your plants with the design established for the hardscape. It is also quicker, simplifies ordering later on, and makes correcting easier as you go along.

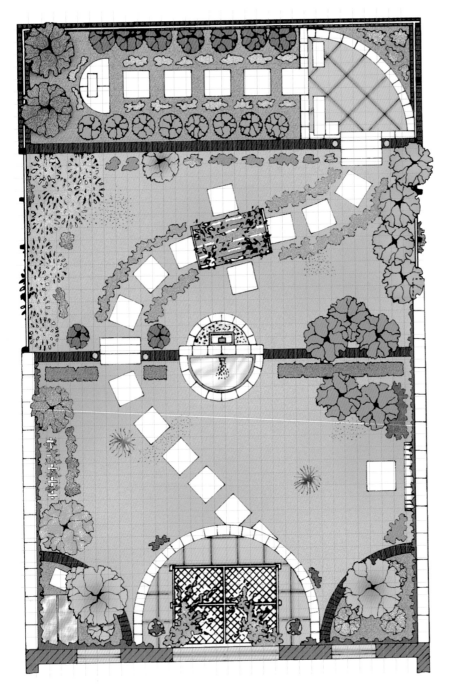

1 square = 1 foot

Fig. 4-5b. Step 3.
Design illusion techniques
In order to maintain the
scaled proportions of the
design as the garden
matures, note that trees and
shrubs are small-height
types, slow growing, or lend
themselves to pruning (or are
a combination of all three).
Vines are the exception,
because of the rapid
coverage desired for vertical
and overhead planes and for
screening. Most plants have
a light/airy foliage texture or
open growth habit for the
recessive value they provide.
Note also the absence of
overplanting, and the value
of mainly perimeter planting,
which leaves more openness
in the center, further
reinforcing the illusion of
greater space.

Step 3: The Plantscape and Finished Design

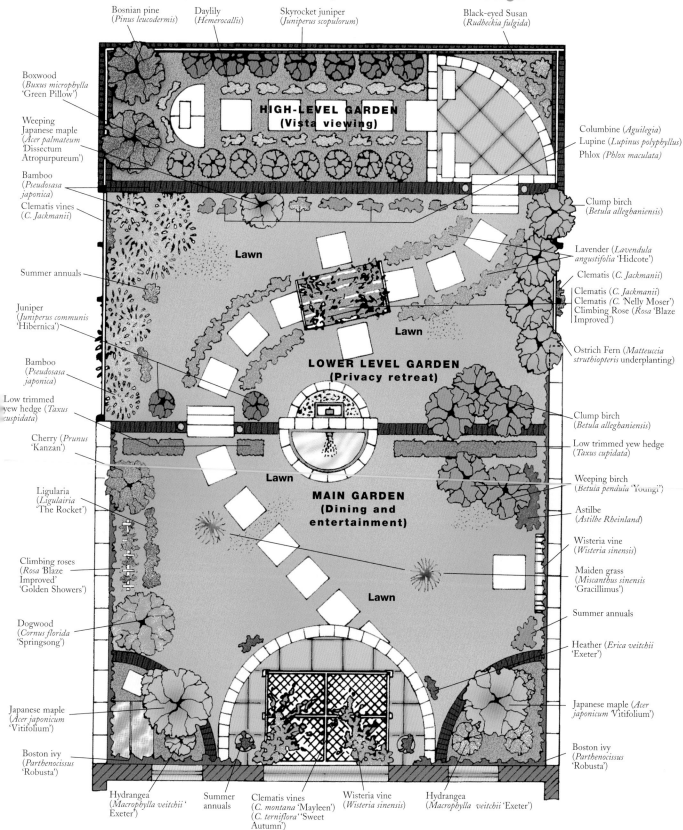

Bosnian pine (*Pinus leucodermis*)

Daylily (*Hemerocallis*)

Skyrocket juniper (*Juniperus scopulorum*)

Black-eyed Susan (*Rudbeckia fulgida*)

Boxwood (*Buxus microphylla* 'Green Pillow')

Weeping Japanese maple (*Acer palmateum* 'Dissectum Atropurpureum')

Bamboo (*Pseudosasa japonica*)

Clematis vines (*C. Jackmanii*)

Summer annuals

Juniper (*Juniperus communis* 'Hibernica')

Bamboo (*Pseudosasa japonica*)

Low trimmed yew hedge (*Taxus cuspidata*)

Cherry (*Prunus* 'Kanzan')

Ligularia (*Ligulairia* 'The Rocket')

Climbing roses (*Rosa* 'Blaze Improved' 'Golden Showers')

Dogwood (*Cornus florida* 'Springsong')

Japanese maple (*Acer japonicum* 'Vitifolium')

Boston ivy (*Parthenocissus* 'Robusta')

Hydrangea (*Macrophylla veitchii* 'Exeter')

Summer annuals

Clematis vines (*C. montana* 'Mayleen') (*C. terniflora* "Sweet Autumn")

Wisteria vine (*Wisteria sinensis*)

Hydrangea (*Macrophylla veitchii* 'Exeter')

HIGH-LEVEL GARDEN (Vista viewing)

Columbine (*Aguilegia*)

Lupine (*Lupinus polyphyllus*)

Phlox (*Phlox maculata*)

Clump birch (*Betula alleghaniensis*)

Lavender (*Lavendula angustifolia* 'Hidcote')

Clematis (*C. Jackmanii*)

Clematis (*C. Jackmanii*) Clematis (*C. Nelly Moser*) Climbing Rose (*Rosa* 'Blaze Improved')

Ostrich Fern (*Matteuccia struthiopteris* underplanting)

Clump birch (*Betula alleghaniensis*)

Low trimmed yew hedge (*Taxus cupidata*)

Weeping birch (*Betula pendula* 'Youngi')

Astilbe (*Astilbe Rheinland*)

Wisteria vine (*Wisteria sinensis*)

Maiden grass (*Miscanthus sinensis* 'Gracillimus')

Summer annuals

Heather (*Erica veitchii* 'Exeter')

Japanese maple (*Acer japonicum* 'Vitifolium')

Boston ivy (*Parthenocissus* 'Robusta')

Lawn

LOWER LEVEL GARDEN (Privacy retreat)

Lawn

MAIN GARDEN (Dining and entertainment)

Lawn

As you examine the Step 3 plan, you will find two points of note. The first is the explanation accompanying the plan, revealing how the plants achieve the design illusion techniques that meet the needs of this particular design. Second, as you scan the entire area, note how the placement of the plants emphasizes the feeling of more to come in the garden, rather than blocking out each individual level.

As with the hardscape, it is best to follow a logical sequence as you begin adding your selected plants to the plan. Start by drawing in the dominant and more important trees that reinforce the main shapes of the garden design. For example, using the Step 3 sample drawing as a reference, put in such trees as pine, birch, cherry, dogwood, bamboo, and juniper; note that these are mainly around the perimeter, as are most of the climbing vines (Boston ivy, clematis, etc.), for screening and coverage. Then, moving inward, begin to plot in the smaller shrubs—Japanese maple and hydrangea—along with the low hedges of boxwood and yew that separate the three levels or rooms of the garden. Finally, add the perennials such as daylily, ferns, and lavender to the meandering edges of the lawn, to surround the clumps of trees or reinforce the main lines of the hardscape.

With all the parts (landscape and plantscape tracing overlaid together), the finished garden plan is now complete, and it is time to sit back and review. Check that all the elements fit and blend together as a total unit. Compare the new plan against the original garden (Step 1) to ensure that you have achieved the feeling of a larger space and are making maximum use of the illusion techniques. Comparing the two versions at this stage will go a long way toward assuring yourself that this has been achieved.

Don't be discouraged if drafting or drawing is not your forte. You are not trying to create a masterpiece on paper. It is a means to an end—creating a beautiful garden. Provided careful scaling is followed, you can succeed.

Although the planning stages shown here are in color and capture the realism of a finished garden, if your own black-and-white line drawing is unsuccessful at evoking the look, feel, and atmosphere of the garden you want to create, remember it is only a road map, not your final destination.

Continue visualizing your garden. Go back to the pictures and photos that influenced you when you were deciding on the elements you wanted in your garden. Revisiting this artwork can give you a renewed sense of the overall garden plan and give you reassurance if your confidence in the design begins to flag.

It is quite common for even the most carefully drawn plan to require some fine tuning, and this is the time to do it. The plan will be your guide for installing the garden in the next step of the process.

chapter five / **installing the garden**

from design to reality
building the garden

installing the garden is a little like launching a new adventure. You have, of course, acted as your own landscape architect. With the plan completed, you are ready to meet the challenge of turning your design into reality by now changing hats to become your own landscape contractor as well. You are like an artist translating the finished sketch to an actual painting, or a sculptor, to a piece of sculpture. As a gardener tending a seed through to a beautiful and dazzling blossom, you can enjoy the artistic rewards of physically building the garden, and this can equal the pleasure of viewing the finished garden itself.

As you begin, you will quickly become aware of the value of an accurately scaled and proportioned plan. Not only is it your shopping list of the right materials and plants—the pieces that must live together in harmony (Fig. 5–2)—the plan will continue to keep you disciplined during the installation of the garden.

Getting Approval

But first things first. Before embarking on purchases and construction, be sure to determine that your design meets with any local guidelines and regulations that may exist. While it is

Fig. 5-1 (preceding page). Full planting goes a long way toward creating the illusion of a larger garden. Here, underplanting of perennials (daylilies on the right) and other small trailing plants under larger trees makes the best possible use of every available square inch, while retaining the maximum living space.

ironic that we garden to relax and escape the outside world of urban
restrictions and controls, we are not immune to the yoke of
bureaucracy. It can follow us into the garden like a bug or a slug.

As a rule, ground level gardens are free from controls, and
prior approval is usually not necessary. It's a good idea to take a
look at what has been done in surrounding gardens, particularly
when it comes to fences. If you have any doubt, check with your
local authorities to be sure. As a courtesy, you might also want to
let your neighbor know your plans.

**Fig. 5-2. In a finished garden,
the right plants and structures
blend harmoniously to
reinforce the vista.**

Fig. 5-3. It pays to get a
jump start if you don't mind
the weather.

Aboveground gardens on rooftops, terraces, etc., however, present an entirely different situation, because of the added weight and the potential damage and leaks that can occur if not properly installed. Here it's not just the plants that are introduced, but also the heavy soil containers in which they grow. Get prior approval in writing of any plan before buying any plants and materials and before beginning any construction. Many apartment buildings issue guidelines for adding gardens, and most use a structural engineer or architect in the approval process to ensure a sound installation. If the garden is on the roof of your own home, consult an architect familiar with your type of building.

When to Start

The best time to begin installing the garden is late March or early April, or even sooner if you are the hardy, outdoors type. Try to get a head start and begin by installing the hardscape first, so that it is complete by the time the last frost for your area has passed and the growing season for the planting begins. It's never too soon to start, even if you are caught by late-season snow flurries when the lumber is delivered to your roof garden (Fig. 5–3). Spring is by far the best time for most planting; the maximum growth occurs at this time and it is at its most vigorous, so plants have a chance to get well-established before the heat of summer and well before the harshness of winter; these two seasonal extremes are exaggerated even more the higher the garden is from the ground. Apart from any stress on the plants, there will be far less heat stress on you as you go about your work setting up the garden, and you will be able to enjoy the results of your efforts in the summertime, rather than waiting another year.

Getting Organized

If you have never built a garden before, you have many things to consider for the construction to run as smoothly as possible. It is inevitable in creating any new project for a certain amount of chaos to result. This is quite normal. Fig. 5–4 serves as an example of what can happen when you are building a deck on a rooftop garden; the agility of a mountain goat is required until the flooring is completed. Only then can plants begin appearing, as space allows (Fig. 5–5).

It's possible to minimize the chaos and make the task much easier by getting organized and following a logical sequence of steps. This is essential for working in the restrictive confines of a small garden space in which you are going to build and install, especially if the plan involves the addition of vertical and overhead items to create the feeling of a fuller, more expansive space.

A preliminary step in getting organized is to check for access to the garden plot. If you have followed the scaled design procedure in Chapter Four, you will have some idea of the size of the hardscape items and plants you have planned for your own

garden space. Do not overlook the delivery access route in your enthusiasm to get started. Most often in the case of a small garden, delivery access can mean going through a narrow, confined area to reach the backyard or up an elevator or flight of stairs to a rooftop or terrace garden. Do check first that the material will fit through. While it may be a source of amusement to friends and neighbors to see you stranded on the curbside with a mountain of material, it is no laughing matter to you when it actually happens.

Site Preparation

The design example in Chapter Four should be used as a guide from here on for everything that is to follow in the installation. The first thing to do is to prepare the site.

Clear the space of all existing items, such as old trees and shrubs, ground roots, any rocks, paving, or old fencing. Dispose of everything you will not be reusing in the new design. Then roughly regrade the ground surface to the three levels in preparation for the new design.

Fig. 5-4 (above, left). Despite the best planning, chaos is to be expected while constructing most small gardens.

Fig. 5-5 (above, right). Once the flooring is complete, plants and planting material can be brought in.

The space is now ready. Remember that in a small garden with hardly any space left unoccupied, you need every square inch to work in. There is something very positive in starting with an open space or canvas, but from here on, prepare for clutter until you complete your masterpiece.

Selecting Materials

In selecting materials for the hardscape, choose only those that can withstand rain, dampness, the freeze/thaw cycle, and whatever else is typical of your climate. Choosing this way will lengthen the life of your structures. While brick, cement, concrete pavers, and stone are fine, iron for arches is subject to rust unless coated or galvanized, and tiles, unless specially made for outdoor use, are subject to cracking from frost. Cedar and redwood are excellent choices for outdoor wooden structures, including planters. These woods are the most readily available from the lumberyard, are economical, last well, and are easy to work with. Cedar, in particular, is useful because it dries rapidly (because of its highly porous, breathable fibers), and is exceptionally light—an important point when weight is a consideration. Pine, although probably the cheapest wood, should be avoided due to its tendency to rot. Teak has excellent lasting qualities but is very expensive and very tough for carpentry work. And, finally, use only galvanized or non-ferrous nails, screws, and bolts in the construction.

Beginning the Hardscape

Begin the installation with all the items that require masonry work and complete the floor area first. Hold off on the delivery of any lumber or plants, since you need an open site to mark off the position of each part of the hardscape as well and room for building. Using the design example as a guide, first install the separating walls and steps for the three different levels. Your tools at this point will be the spade, builder's trowel, and most important, the level, measuring tape, and string to accurately mark out the areas carefully scaled proportionate to the hardscape drawing. Build the fountain and the dry well for drainage, then complete the surrounding walls of the High-Level Garden and the curved brick planting beds of the Main Garden. The remaining paved living area under the arbor and on the vista viewing platform are then laid, along with the paved curved paths that link the garden together and provide the flow.

With the floor work completed, you will still have an open working area and the space for delivery and storage of the lumber (see Figs. 5–6 and 5–7). Continue next with all the carpentry items in the design example—the shade arbor, storage shed, trellis fencing for screening and vine support, framed wall mirror for the illusion of the garden extending beyond, benches, metal arch arbor, and rose support. All woodwork is stained in an off-white or light beige color for its recessive value, though it still retains the definition and shape essential to the overall design. Finally, installation of the pump for the fountain completes the hardscape portion of the installation in a typical ground-level backyard space.

If your space is aboveground and part of a building (eg., rooftop, penthouse, or terrace) and has a finished floor surface, the masonry step would be bypassed and you would begin with the lumber item. With your approved plan in hand (see "Getting Approval," page 84), you can begin work. The key difference between a backyard garden and one above ground is that here

all your structures are modular. Everything is movable, allowing inspection and roof maintenance work when necessary. At the same time, all your items should be firmly anchored in position for safety. They must be able to withstand winds, which can become much stronger the higher the garden is situated. This semipermanence allows flexibility and temporary removal and eventual reinstallation in sections as necessary, avoiding a complete remake of the garden when any roof repairs are made.

Follow a construction sequence similar to the one previously described for ground-level design. Begin by building and installing any decking in your plan, making it in about 4-by-6-foot sections for easy removal. Make sure the sections are elevated with supports that allow free runoff of moisture below. Follow this with any major structures such as the arbor, lag-bolted together and firmly bolted to vertical walls as they rest on the deck (using bolts makes for easy dismantling if necessary). Add the vertical trellis or fencing, again anchored to be wind resistant and also made up of about 4- by- 6-foot bolted sections. The planters, taking the

Fig. 5-6 (above, left). Keep the site as orderly as possible once work is underway.

Fig. 5-7 (above, right). Having a flat, open surface will speed the process and ensure greater accuracy.

place of the ground, will form the bulk of the carpentry work. A good size is a 24-inch cube with a weight of about 40 pounds per square foot when filled, manageable to move, and within most weightloading requirements. The planters should be elevated on legs to allow unimpeded water run-off, to guard against rotting, and prevent any penetrating root damage as the garden matures.

Whether you have a backyard or an aboveground space, once the hardscape has been completed, double-check everything for safety and practicality one last time before adding the plants. Make sure you have kept to any approval requirements and regulations, ensure that major structures are sturdily built and secure (especially on high), and finally, review your usage and living areas, to verify that any dining or garden furniture you may have in mind will fit.

Hardscape Contractor Option

While the planting part (see "Planting the Plantscape," page 94) of the design should be well within the realm of most keen gardeners (love of plants is, after all, why we garden), not all of us are blessed with the dexterity and knowledge of even some of the simpler structural skills of a mason or carpenter. The market is full of easy-to-understand and inexpensive self-help booklets on the subject. If you are capable or adventurous, fine. If not, you may wish to consider hiring a landscape contractor to carry out this part of the project under your close supervision.

A good way to find a contractor is to approach a local plant nursery or garden center, preferably a large one with a good reputation. Most sizable ones have their own contracting service with their own staff; if not, they should be able to recommend a reliable source. The ideal, of course, would be to use the same plant nursery you order your plants from, since they would likely be more conscientious, to avoid jeopardizing your plant order. It is essential that your contractor draw up shop plans (detailed scaled drawing with instructions) before commencing work. Carefully check that the dimensions, proportions, and positioning on these plans match those on your own plan, since your contractor may not be familiar with the importance of the accuracy required by the space illusion techniques you are using.

Soil Preparation

Inevitably, all the hardscape activity will leave the soil in a sorry, compacted state as you come close to the final planting stage. Soil is your most valuable asset for making the garden flourish, so the next step is to prepare and redeem the beds for planting. Make sure the soil has a balanced pH level of about 6.5 (not too acidic, not too alkaline), amend with organic matter to make the soil more friable (crumbly), and add a mix of balanced 5–10–5 fertilizer (nitrogen for foliage, phosphorus for flowers, and potash for all-around vigor and healthy root growth). Dig in the nutrients and loosen the soil well. If your plot is similar to the example, with large, overgrown trees and shrubs, chances are your garden has not been fed in a long time and the soil is almost totally depleted of food from the heavy root mass. Soil quality becomes even more critical if yours is an all-planter garden since the roots are totally confined within the planter and cannot spread and seek out sources from a wider area. Here it is better to use an equal mix of vermiculite, peat moss, and soil, not only for lighter weight, but for greater moisture and nutrient retention.

Planting the Plantscape

The final step to make the transformation complete is putting the plants into the garden. Plants are the element of the design that brings the whole space to life, and they add equally to the design illusion results by visibly cloaking the area with a light, airy texture. By the time you are ready to plant, about 90 percent of the work will already have been done. Adding the plants should be the easy part and should take very little time.

Planting, like the previous stages of garden building, is best handled by following a logical sequence. While the plant selection and positioning on your own plan may vary, the sample plan for the backyard space will serve as a commonsense guide. Begin planting around the outer perimeter of the garden, starting with the major trees and plants such as dogwood, cherry, bamboo, juniper, clump birch, weeping birch, and finally Japanese maple; complete the perimeter by adding the screening vines such as clematis, Boston ivy, and roses. This frees up the central area for the smaller shrubs of weeping Japanese maple and hydrangea, and the low boxwood and trimmed yew hedges, to separate the three sections of the garden without disturbing the main plants already in place. It also minimizes the risk of trampling the more tender perennials and annuals as you work.

The sequence is now more flexible as the remaining plants are positioned. Annuals and perennials can now be planted. Plant annuals in beds and in pots, followed by perennials such as ligularia, daylily, columbine, lavender, fern, and astilbe. Then plant wisteria and clematis for the shade arbor, along with climbing roses and clematis for the arched arbor in the lower level garden. Finally, sow or sod the lawn, with ornamental grasses added to

complete the planting for the design. Once established, the lawn
can be edged so it follows and echoes the shapes of the planting
beds to give definition.

If your design is an all-planter terrace or rooftop, the same
basic planting sequence applies, except that planting the restrictive
small soil surface would be completed at the same time. This
includes everything that is to go in the same planter, from trees,
shrubs, and underplanting of the perennials.

The transition from design to reality is now complete.
You have transformed a small urban space into what feels like a
larger and more complete garden (Fig. 5-8). To quote painter and
garden designer Gertrude Jekyll, "The size of a garden has very
little to do with its merit. It is merely an accident relating to the
circumstances of the owner. It is the size of his heart and brain
and goodwill that make his garden . . . that of a work of fine art."

**Fig. 5–8. Take pride in your
garden of delights.**

chapter six / **garden structures**

an unlimited
range of possibilities

while the range of garden structures is practically unlimited, the types and their usage depend on your own individual taste, the function they have to perform, and how they reinforce the garden style and blend in with the design you are creating. And although all sizes of garden can and do benefit from the visual interest and the framework the structures provide to hold the garden together, their value is magnified when faced with the task of "enlarging" a small space garden.

There are two reasons. The first is that structures are the most visible and thus are one of the main means (along with plants) of creating the illusion of greater space by the technique of proportionate reduction. The other is that when used for vertical and overhead support of foliage, they take better advantage of normally unused air space, thereby creating the same feeling commonly associated in the mind with a larger size garden.

When deciding on the number of structures to use, it is important to strike a balance. Too few will fall short of achieving the illusion; too many will create clutter and have the reverse effect, working against spaciousness. When choosing the style, be sure to keep it constant throughout all the structures for a

Fig. 6-1 (preceding page). Even the narrowest of spaces (30 inches wide) can bring charm and interest to the entrance path of the garden. Weeping birches create a unique appearance of light, airy foliage. The alley effect is completed by a drift of yellow daylilies below—one method of adding extra plants though not in the main garden.

Fig. 6-2 (opposite). Harmony in structural style of the hardscape helps capture and unite seemingly disparate areas to expand the small garden. Here, the midlevel roof area is linked to the viewing platform, with the lines of skylight continuing into the small shady space below, combining the gardens for the impression of a far larger and more expansive space.

harmonious flow; lack of unity can be jarring and quickly erode the visual effect.

This townhouse garden (Fig. 6-2) is a good example of how a harmonious fit helps create a continuous flow, in this case, between the various levels. In addition to using many of the types of garden structures that follow in the next few pages, it demonstrates how structures, combined properly, can unify the different sections to create the appearance of a much larger garden than would initially seem possible with just a restrictive 20-by-20-foot roof space. Starting at the top is a shade arbor styled to give a cozy, secluded feel at the entry to the main deck area, edged at the sides with flowering vines on the trellis fence. The deck is at two levels with sunken planters and staged at the back to carry a copper-lined rill fed with a row of water spouts reminiscent of the famous "Alley of the Hundred Fountains," Villa d'Este, Tivoli (the water feature is not visible from this angle). The middle area follows, taking the form of a "widow's walk" platform (a place where whalers' wives would wait for their husbands to return from the

Fig. 6-3. Sound fence anchorage and structural stability are top priorities. They protect the fence from high winds, which are prevalent on rooftops.

sea) set in a line of narrow junipers, opening up the vista of the neighboring gardens down below for a feel of expansiveness and extra borrowed enjoyment. Finally, following the lines of the angled skylight are the unifying spars of the narrow all-shade ground-level garden, completing the design.

The following are just some of the more common structures that make up the hardscape, and they are briefly described in terms of their attributes, along with an indication of how they work to enlarge the space. If they spark ideas for your own garden design for a better fit, be sure to embellish whatever you decide to adapt or create with the architectural style of your home or the other dominant features that surround your plot.

Fences

Fences help frame the garden and hold it together by giving the design overall shape and definition. They help screen out unsightly views, provide privacy, and offer protection from the wind. Their strongest illusion attribute for a small garden is that they provide support for vine growth on the vertical plane, thereby allowing a greater amount of foliage and flowers than would normally be expected.

With a the board-and-board type fence (Fig. 6-3), the intent is to provide privacy from the neighboring rooftop garden, but at the same time prevent drag from damaging high winds by allowing air to pass between the alternating boards. Quite different again is the narrow vertical lath fence and gate (Fig. 6-4), which shows how the fence alone, even without vines, not only echoes the Japanese style garden within but adds a light, airy touch for a feeling of expansiveness.

Fig. 6-4. A fence can add more than just a perimeter boundary alone; it can also reinforce the design within.

Trellis

The trellis is perhaps the most versatile of all items when it comes to small gardens. It can be functional, decorative, and illusion-enhancing, depending on where it is used. It can be an alternative to more standard-type fences, provide dappled shade when used with an arbor, cover an unsightly brick wall, and even decorate planters, obelisks, and arches. Its most important value when painted white is its lacy, recessive value, creating an illusion of greater openness; and it provides vertical and overhead vine support.

An example of trellis versatility (Fig. 6-5) shows how the trellis both frames the windows—adding interest to a dull stretch of wall—and compensates for the narrow floor space with flowering vines and climbers on the vertical plane.

In this same garden (Fig. 6-6) it is also used as a fence support for espaliered juniper, creating a green wall without the use of plant-support stakes for stability. Trellis is also used on top of the arbor. When used to train newly planted wisteria, it adds significantly to planting on the overhead plane.

Fig. 6-5 (opposite). The decorative qualities of a trellis can bring a dull wall to life.

Fig. 6-6 (above). A trellis is ideal for creating foliage support on both the vertical and overhead planes.

Decking

Because decking can create different levels and bring more drama and interest to the garden, it helps to divert the eye away from the smallness of the space. The illusion is further enhanced when the deck is made of light silvery-gray cedar, which brings a feeling of openness, especially when the deck is the largest structure in the garden. Decking is also useful for emphasizing other structures, such as a dining area or viewing platform, and in practical terms, it protects or simply conceals an unsightly roof surface.

This particular townhouse rooftop (Fig. 6-7) shows an example of a second-level raised deck. It also functions as an unusually spacious sitting area to spread out on, sharing space with a carved swan and potted specimen plant.

Paving

Paving is by far the most effective method of covering heavy-traffic areas where a grass surface would be either impractical or vulnerable to continuous damage. Paving works particularly well under arbors, dining or seating areas, and viewing platforms and provides a stable surface for benches and tables. When used in paths, paving helps make a strong visual transition between the various sections of the garden. At the same time, it helps unify them and gives flow to the garden as a whole. Paved edging around flower beds, particularly when the beds are raised, also works well by adding definition to the individual shapes and giving them increased presence.

While pavers come ready-made, in this particular example of work in progress (Fig. 6-8), the cement pavers were colored

Fig. 6-7 (top). A place to sit and rest and perhaps showcase one of your favorite plants.

Fig. 6-8 (bottom). Casting your own pavers can sometimes be the only way to get the results you strive for.

and cast on site, then laid on a concrete base. They were tinted to reinforce the Mediterranean mood of the garden. They form the central circle and gathering point of the design.

The stone character of paving adds a desirable natural touch to any garden, as seen in Fig. 6-9, where it is used to edge a lily pond and provide a small bridge.

Fig. 6-9. Paving brings the naturalness of stone for better definition of shapes.

Arches

Arches are fun and provide a charming touch to any garden, but particularly a small-space one, because of the diversionary allure and interest they create. Perhaps their appeal is a carryover from our childhood days, when a den or tunnel was a magical place to hide or play. In any case, they successfully punctuate the transition from one garden section to another, as shown by the metal arches cloaked in clematis on this narrow terrace (Fig. 6-10). And notice in the second variation (Fig. 6-11) how the arch is styled to echo the architectural apex of the parapet wall as the corner is turned, for a good fit.

But most of all, the prime benefit in terms of space is that arches provide the means for additional vertical and overhead vining foliage and flowers to enhance the illusion of a larger garden.

Fig. 6-10 (above). Arches always add fascinating interest and create extra space for more flowers and foliage.

Fig. 6-11 (opposite). The arbor not only introduces another part of the garden, it blends in with the coping stone behind, creating structural harmony.

Arbors

An arbor has long been a favorite in many gardens and often becomes the natural gathering point, a little like an inglenook in the days of yore. It satisfies the same needs for a cozy, private retreat, only this time outdoors in the beauty of nature. An arbor's symbolic association with expansive pastures, perhaps more than any other type of structure, psychologically reinforces the feeling and illusion of a larger urban garden space.

Because of its relatively large size—and therefore its visibility—an arbor can make a dominant contribution to the design when it blends in with the surrounding architecture and can even lend itself to a bit of theatrical styling to captivate the interest level further. Because it is so prominent, its proportionate reduction must be calculated very accurately to keep it in scale proportionate with the other garden elements.

The cool and enclosed atmosphere of the arbor shown in Fig. 6-12 is created by enveloping the structure with wisteria vines against a walled backdrop of Boston ivy, making it the perfect

Fig. 6-12. One benefit of an arbor is the respite it provides from sun and wind exposure.

shady retreat or alcove for dining. A different use for an arbor is shown in Fig. 6-13, where it is designed totally as a privacy screen for both the garden and the apartment itself from an immediately facing towering apartment complex. The vertical evergreen ilex

Fig. 6-13. Privacy is often a consideration in a closely knit high-rise urban district.

shrubs and narrowly spaced trellis above are linked by the curved architectural upright spars, ensuring year-round escape from the typical urban garden phenomena of close living and prying eyes.

The primary attribute in space-illusion terms of an arbor is that it provides the framework to introduce foliage on both the vertical and horizontal planes.

Planters

By far the most important attribute of planters is in their ability to provide the means to create a small urban garden when in-ground planting is not an option. Planters make it possible for many urban gardens to exist—and allow plants to grow and flourish as they would in conventional earthbound circumstances. At ground level, a patio or very small backyard may be either totally or mostly paved over to ensure adequate living space, with little or no room to create an in-ground garden. High above the ground, on a terrace or rooftop, no planting space exists at all on the concrete or tiled surface. So planters are vital in small and urban gardens aboveground.

Of all garden structures, only in planters is scaled reduction for illusion purposes secondary; the primary emphasis is on the size necessary for the growing needs of the plants. However, great choice exists regarding style and shape. For example, planters can have a clean and simple design (Fig. 6-14) to blend in with the overall style or narrow width of the garden. Alternatively, even if they are square or oblong, they can be clustered behind a rounded and curved fascia (Fig. 6-15) for greater interest and to break up the formality of the square shape.

Fig. 6-14 (opposite, top). Plant needs and available width determine planter size and shape.

Fig. 6-15 (opposite, bottom). Square (or oblong) planters can be clustered, where space permits, behind a curved false fascia.

III

Water Features

Since the time of ancient Mesopotamia, water features and gardens have been synonymous with places of beauty and pleasure. As the very source of life itself, water continues to hold enchantment and fascination for both young and old alike. Such appeal makes water features an almost perfect point of focus to draw the eye away from the size of the garden plot. And a water feature can be any shape and style you wish to make it, provided it is in harmony with the garden design. Water features are varied and include waterfalls, ponds, and fountains.

Something as simple and elegant as a terra-cotta pot with a small bubble jet, placed on an ivy-covered base and flanked with weeping spruce (Fig. 6-16), serves as a peaceful centerpiece: the pot itself amplifies the sound of the water, muffling the roar of urban traffic below.

Fig. 6-16. Basking in the sight and sound of water can be an unrivaled pleasure.

Different entirely is the fountain where water spurts from
the mouth of Bacchus (the mythical god of revelry) into a stone
trough (Fig. 6-17). With the mask mounted on a framed mirror
encased in white trellis, the intention was to overcome the narrow
4-foot-wide ground-level garden space. When the facing glass
entry doors are open, both sight and tranquil sound of water enter
the living space, which also lends a feeling of greater depth to
the outside perimeter of the garden. While it is not unusual for
a water feature to provide the pleasures of running water, it is
unusual for the setting in which it is housed to simultaneously
create the illusion of greater depth in opposing directions.

**Fig. 6-17. The mythic face
on this water feature adds
interest and whimsy.**

Floor Mosaics

Floors mosaics have long held a place in garden history, and as a form of embellishment they are a useful means of bringing additional interest to an otherwise plain floor area without taking up additional space. Over and above their value as a diversion—they detract the eye from the smallness of space—their greatest value is in enhancing and reinforcing the design of the garden. For example, if your garden relies heavily on trellises or vines, a simple scene depicting flowering clematis would work well; you can portray topiary if your garden style is formal. Whatever subject you decide on, choose colors from the flowers in the garden for harmony and relevance.

In Fig. 6-18, the theme chosen for the mosaic is based on the Duke of Montefeltro's crest and his liberal arts studiolo

Fig. 6-18. Mosaics are an excellent medium for capturing the garden theme.

(a library or place of learning) built at Gubbio, in 15th-century Italy, on which the overall garden design is based. The studiolo itself was transported from Italy and is now on permanent display at New York's Metropolitan Museum of Art. The garden serves as an outdoor extension to a children's library and school. The quest for knowledge and the desire to educate young minds are just as relevant now as in the days of the Renaissance.

This further example (Fig. 6-19) of a cathedral rose window (here, enclosing a fountain) is an interpretation of the actual window of the cathedral where the garden is located. This example shows it centrally positioned, the highlight of the design.

Fig. 6-19. The right subject takes full advantage of the architecture of the building.

Pots and Urns

Despite their relatively small size, pots and urns are valuable and versatile in the contribution they make to the small-space garden. In some cases they are the only option available to make a garden possible—for example, in a small balcony, where light weight and small size are necessary. However, their main value in all types of small gardens is that they are a source of extra summer color from annuals and tropicals, in addition to the main flower beds. Flowers are the main source of color in any garden, and light pastels in particular help reinforce the desired feeling of greater openness.

Pots and urns are extremely versatile because they are easily transported and can be rotated. Flowers at their peak of bloom can be given pride of place in the garden. And they can be placed almost anywhere. The pot of begonias with a miniature rose (Fig. 6-20) is positioned to recapture some of the space lost to the floor surface. Similarly, an urn can be used as a sentinel in various parts of the garden, or even flank the front steps to the house itself (Fig. 6-21) as a welcome and a hint of what is to follow in the backyard garden.

The main overall illusion effect of pots and urns is to brighten up the small summer garden while allowing a disproportionate amount of extra plants without the feeling of intrusiveness or crowding.

Fig. 6-20 (opposite). Pots lend colorful support to the main players and give more places to plant.

Fig. 6-21 (above). An urn can adorn and further enhance a prominent spot in the garden.

Other Garden Structures

The list of garden structures is practically endless. Some more common ones include sculpture, bird feeders, birdbaths, and obelisks, as seen in Fig. 6-22, (to echo and visually unite the garden with the skyline vista), benches, sundials, and even combined greenhouse/ garden sheds. Some types of structures may not even

Fig. 6-22. An obelisk brings the vertical background grandeur into the garden.

be available commercially, but will come to light in your imagination, for instance, this vine-covered pew-styled seat (Fig. 6-23). If you get an inkling of an original idea that can add a distinctive and personal touch to your garden creation, by all means pursue the thought, provided the structure will enhance the visual illusion and blend in with the design.

Fig. 6-23. While waiting for the spring vines to enfold a covered pew, this is a delightful spot to escape the hot summer sun.

chapter seven / **plants**

the right plant
for the right place

most of us have a reasonable knowledge of the more commonly used plants from working in our own gardens, visits to plant nurseries, excursions to other prominent gardens, and even from the regular flood of plant catalogs we receive in late winter every year that rekindle our enthusiasm. In choosing the right plant for the right place in the garden, we have learned to consider such things as cold hardiness, amount of sun or shade, annual rainfall, and other general factors.

But when it comes to creating illusion in the small urban garden, we have a whole new set of factors to consider. We need to be more focused on plant selection in two main ways: choosing plants that will directly contribute to the feeling of having a garden larger than it really is (design illusion attributes), and choosing plants that will adapt to the different types of space that are available for small urban gardens (growing requirements).

So in the selection process we have to narrow down the seemingly endless range of plant types found in larger and more spacious gardens to meet the criteria. This is somewhat akin to Darwin's Theory of Natural Selection, only in this case we take over from nature.

Fig. 7-1 (preceding page). A closely and fully planted (but not overcrowded) garden can go a long way toward achieving the feeling of a large, complete garden when it is tucked into a small lot.

Fig. 7-2 (opposite). Blue spruce typifies the light color and texture of many conifers. It is hardy in cold, windy climates.

However, selecting from a much narrower range of choices is not as difficult as it might appear at first glance. Many trees that are thought of as large are also available in small versions. Juniper, for instance, has about 60 species and hundreds of cultivars in practically every size, texture, and color. And with limited exception, a similar wide diversity in form exists within many other species in the plant kingdom. Then there are the mainly small-size trees of the genus Prunus, which contains many flowering trees such as cherry, almond, plum, and pear, to mention a few.

Because of the natural tendency to treat the hardscape and plants as two distinct entities, it is important to remember that the two work together to achieve the end result—the feeling of a larger garden. Provided both areas have the same basic illusion characteristics, the methods are interchangeable. For example, to delineate the property line, an evergreen hedge may be preferred over a fence; small shrubs rather than low brick walls can separate different parts of the garden; vines or trellises make high walls equally recessive. Bear this in mind when choosing plants in your garden design.

To help in the selection process, a list of the more familiar plants—trees, shrubs, climbers, perennials, annuals, and tropicals—that are suitable for small-space garden illusion is contained in the Appendix. While the list is not exhaustive, it will serve as a guide. Make a note of plants you come across in your gardening travels, particularly if some of your favorites are among them.

The plants on the list are assessed individually in two main ways: first by their design attributes (ability to aid in creating an illusion), and then by their corresponding required growing conditions (ability to flourish).

Fig. 7-3 (opposite). The small shimmering leaves of clump birch add a sense of increased openness and spaciousness within a small space.

Design Attributes

The number and type of design attributes listed in the Appendix vary according to the category and individual type of plant named. Both the common and botanical names of plants are given.

For example in the conifer category, the needlelike leaves of spruce have a light, airy texture (Fig. 7-2), while narrow, upright junipers add vertical plane growth, and yews take well to pruning for control of size and shape of hedges separating garden segments.

Clump birch (Fig. 7-3), under the deciduous trees category, also bring a light texture, while cherry and crab bring pastel colors with their springtime burst of flowers.

In the category of evergreen shrubs, small boxwood (Fig. 7-4) is both slow-growing and easily trimmed, while the low-spreading cotoneaster adds a color bonus of berries to its small-leaf foliage.

All the deciduous shrubs have light pastel flower colors in their range, with hydrangea (Fig. 7-5) as an example. Forsythia heralds the onset of spring with a splash of golden-yellow flowers, while Rose of Sharon draws the curtain on the season with a wide range of light-colored flowers.

Fig. 7-4 (opposite). Boxwood hedge is ideal for maintaining scale and proportion and for reinforcing the shape of beds.

Fig 7-5 (above). The white color of this hydrangea adds to the many light shades of the flower mix, contributing to the receding-border effect.

Climbers as a category have many desirable design attributes. They are the best way to achieve vertical, mostly overhead, plane coverage to better utilize space. Boston ivy, climbing hydrangea, and English ivy, for instance, are excellent for covering walls with foliage, while clematis, climbing roses, and wisteria (Fig. 7-6) have the full range of attributes.

Fig 7-6. Climbers like wisteria are ideal candidates for the vertical and overhead planes.

Most plants in the perennial category provide a wide range of pastel or light, recessive colors: for example, astilbe, daylily, and goldenrod, while others such as columbine and fern (Fig. 7-7) provide light, airy foliage texture. The grass category also has the qualities of airy texture, as shown by striped eulalia (Fig. 7-8). Bamboo can also contribute height.

Fig. 7-7 (top). The delicate fronds of ferns are a natural for their airy quality.

Fig. 7-8 (bottom). The narrow blades of ornamental grass could be a horticultural version of a light starburst.

Seasonal annuals such as impatiens (Fig. 7-9) are an ideal way to bring light pastel flower color into the garden to best make the space appear to recede, giving maximum openness to even the most minuscule garden.

Like annuals, tropicals perform in a similar way with respect to color, but with a brighter and more exotic touch, like that of plumbago (Fig. 7-10) and the showy large blossoms of hibiscus.

Fig. 7-9 (above). Creating a carpet of densely flowering impatiens is just one way of using annuals to establish the color palette.

Fig. 7-10 (opposite). What could be better than azure blue to bring the lightness of the sky and add to the spacious feeling?

Growing Conditions

Small urban spaces have their own special growing conditions, and suitablility of plants for a small garden can vary considerably by garden type and location. These special considerations, listed under "Growing Conditions" in the Appendix, are the focus here.

For example, a glance down the "Takes to Some Crowding" column indicates which plants can compensate for smallish space (provided this is not overdone). Notice that with the exception of four conifers (used for hedging), no other trees are included, neither conifer nor deciduous. Conversely, practically all the plants in the remaining categories are included, mainly because of their small size, provided crowding is not critical or harmful, or where massing gives a pleasing visual effect (Fig. 7-11).

Every plant listed may be adapted for container gardening. It is their small size (of trees, in particular), their slow growth rate, and their ability to balance top growth in direct proportion to restricted root ball size that make them suitable for planters.

While the open ground of a backyard (the most prevalent of spaces) allows for planting directly into the soil, practically all other types of urban garden space are fully paved over or part of the structure of a building, making planters the only way to create a garden. Even backyard gardens benefit when planters extend the garden to areas partially paved over for living and dining.

In the "Pots and Urns" column, only annuals and tropicals qualify, for the obvious reason they do not overwinter or meet the hardiness criteria. Also, the small size of pots leaves little room for the root ball of perennial trees and shrubs and offers insufficient insulation bulk for them or perennials to winter over.

Fig. 7-11 (opposite). Light textured leaves can overcome the feeling of crowdedness.

Every plant on the list (except annuals and tropicals) is hardy enough to survive the coldest winter temperature in a ground-level backyard garden. This means that additional types of plant material can be added to the selection where gardens are located in more moderate climate zones farther south (see the Plant Hardiness Zone Map, page 142).

The plant list for containerized aboveground gardens omits certain ones that may be only marginally hardy in planters. Plants in containers lose the moderating warmth of the ground for the roots and can suffer from the surrounding colder air temperatures that occur. The higher up and farther north the garden is, the harsher the growing conditions become. A good rule of thumb is to build in a safety margin by selecting plants that are rated hardy at least two climate zones north of your area.

The "None Hardy" column is for annuals and tropicals. These are suitable for all types of gardens.

Shade conditions take on extra significance because lack of sun tends to be a factor in small urban backyards. Closely surrounding abutting walls of neighboring houses and nearby high rises—as well as large, self-seeded trees, which can cast dense shade on the garden plot—significantly diminish plant options, particularly when trees play a dominant role in the design of a small garden. Shade is usually not an important factor in container gardens that rise above the ground or in locations that receive at least half a day of sun and quality light the rest of the time.

Some other container garden considerations are not indicated in the chart as growing-conditions columns but are well worth mentioning. In general, growing in planters is always a little more challenging than growing in the ground. In planters,

plants compete for limited resources and are more vulnerable to stress. An exposed planter on a high-rise terrace, for example, can freeze dry in winter, bake dry in summer, and be blow-dried all year round. There's no moderation, so start with mature plants; they are stronger and are better equipped to cope with extremes of temperature. In terms of resources, no natural recycling of nutrients occurs in planters, and the bulk of the rainfall (as much as 80 percent) can be lost down the drain on a paved surface. Be prepared to give nature a helping hand regularly during the growing season by supplying food and moisture. An automatic-drip watering system can be a boon during the sizzling summer months.

Fig. 7-12 (above). The light-pastel flowers of Mandevilla, Coreopsis, and Phlox are versatile, and they brighten the garden. They appear in the plant list in the Appendix.

Overleaf. The flowers of such shade-tolerant plants as hydrangea, astilbe, rhododendron, and begonia make it possible to have light color available for a greater feeling of openness and size even in a small backyard where direct sunlight so often is limited.

appendix

trees and shrubs
suitable for small-space gardens

DESIGN ATTRIBUTES   **GROWING CONDITIONS**

Conifer Trees
(Most available in medium and small tree and shrub sizes, while some others in narrow, spreading, weeping, and dwarf form.)

	Medium/Small Tree	Medium/Small Shrub	Slow-Growing	Takes to Pruning	Light, Airy Texture	Light Pastel Flower Colors	Vertical Plane Growth	Overhead Plane Foliage	Takes Some Crowding	Adapts to Containers	Fine for Pots/Urns	Ground-Level Hardy	Rooftop Hardy	Shade Tolerant
Arborvitae (*Thuja plicata* 'Fastigiata')		●	●	●	●		●		●	●		●	●	
Cedar (*Cedrus libani* 'Sargentii')	●	●	●	●	●					●		●	●	
Cypress (*Chamaecyparis lawsoniana* 'Fletcherii')		●	●	●	●		●			●		●		
Fir (*Abies koreana*)	●	●	●		●					●		●		
Hemlock (*Tsuga canadensis*)		●	●	●	●				●	●		●		●
Juniper (*Juniperus chinensis* 'Obelisk')		●	●	●	●		●		●	●		●	●	●
Pine (*Pinus pinea*)	●	●	●		●					●		●	●	
Spruce (*Picea mariana* 'Doumetii')	●	●	●		●					●		●	●	
Yew (*Yew cuspidata*)		●	●	●			●		●	●		●	●	●
Deciduous Trees														
Birch (*Betula nigra*)	●	●	●	●						●		●	●	
Cherry (*Prunus* 'Kanzan')	●	●	●			●				●		●	●	
Crab (*Malus* 'Profusion')	●	●	●			●				●		●	●	
Dogwood (*Cornus florida* 'Springsong')	●	●	●			●				●		●		●
Golden chain (*Laburnum alpinum*)	●	●	●			●				●		●	●	
Hawthorn (*Crataegus monogynai*)	●	●	●							●		●	●	
Japanese maple (*Acer palmatum* 'Dissectum')	●	●	●	●	●					●		●	●	
Magnolia (*Magnolia stellata*)	●	●	●			●				●		●	●	
Pear (*Pyrus calleryana* 'Chanticleer')	●	●	●							●		●	●	
Redbud (*Cercis siliquastrum*)	●	●	●			●				●		●	●	
Storax (*Styrax officinalis*)	●	●	●		●					●		●		

	MEDIUM/SMALL TREE	MEDIUM/SMALL SHRUB	SLOW-GROWING	TAKES TO PRUNING	LIGHT, AIRY TEXTURE	LIGHT PASTEL FLOWER COLORS	VERTICAL PLANE GROWTH	OVERHEAD PLANE FOLIAGE	TAKES SOME CROWDING	ADAPTS TO CONTAINERS	FINE FOR POTS/URNS	GROUND-LEVEL HARDY	ROOFTOP HARDY	SHADE TOLERANT
Evergreen Shrubs														
Andromeda (*Pieris japonica*)	●	●	●						●	●		●	●	●
Barberry (*Berberis darwinii*)	●	●	●						●	●		●	●	
Boxwood (*Buxus sempervirens*)	●	●	●						●	●		●		●
Burning bush (*Euonymus japonicus*)	●	●	●						●	●		●	●	
Cotoneaster (*Cotoneaster dammeri*)	●	●	●						●	●		●	●	
Firethorn (*Pyracantha watereri*)	●	●	●						●	●		●		
Holly (*Ilex aquifolium*)	●	●	●						●	●		●	●	●
Mountain laurel (*Kalmia latifolia*)	●	●	●			●			●	●		●	●	●
Rhododendron (*Rhododendron* 'Britannia')	●	●	●			●			●	●		●	●	●
Skimmia (*Skimmia japonica*)	●	●	●						●	●		●	●	●
Deciduous Shrubs														
Broom (*Cytisus praecox*)	●	●	●	●	●	●				●		●	●	
Butterfly bush (*Buddlea davidii*)	●	●	●	●		●				●		●	●	
Forsythia (*Forsythia intermedia* 'Spectabilis')	●	●	●	●		●				●		●	●	
Hydrangea (*Hydrangea macrophylla*)	●	●	●			●				●		●		●
Lilac (*Syringa vulgaris*)	●	●	●	●		●				●		●	●	
Rose of Sharon (*Hibiscus syreacus* 'Blue Bird')	●	●	●	●		●				●		●	●	
Viburnum (*Viburnum opulus* 'Sterile')	●	●	●	●		●				●		●		●
Weigela (*Weigela florida* 'Variegate')	●	●	●			●				●		●	●	

vines, perennials, and annuals

Plant	Light Pastel Flower Color	Light Airy Texture	Vertical Plane Growth	Overhead Plane Foliage	Take to Pruning	Takes Some Crowding	Adapts to Containers	Fine for Pots/Urns	Ground-Level Hardy	Rooftop Hardy	None Hardy
Climbers											
Boston ivy (*Parthenocissus tricuspidata*)		●	●		●	●	●		●	●	
Clematis (*Clematis jackmanii*)	●	●	●	●		●	●		●	●	
Climbing hydrangea (*Hydrangea petiolaris*)	●	●	●	●		●	●		●	●	
Climbing rose (*Rosa* 'Blaze')	●	●		●		●	●		●	●	
Dutchmans Pipe (*Aristolochia macrophylla*)			●	●		●	●		●	●	
English ivy (*Hedera helix*)		●		●		●	●		●	●	
Honeysuckle (*Lonicera periclymenum*)	●	●	●	●		●	●		●	●	
Silver lace (*Polygonum aubertii*)	●	●	●		●	●	●		●	●	
Trumpet vine (*Campsis radicans*)	●	●	●	●		●	●		●	●	
Virginia creeper (*Parthenscissus quinquefolia*)		●	●	●	●	●	●		●	●	
Wisteria (*Wisteria sinensis*)	●	●	●	●	●	●	●		●	●	
Perennials											
Astilbe (*Astilbe* 'Pink Lightning')	●	●				●	●		●		
Bamboo (*Phyllostachys aurea*)		●	●		●	●	●		●		
Bleeding heart (*Dicentra eximia* 'Spring Morning')	●	●				●	●		●		
Chrysanthemum (*Chrysanthemum* 'Clara Curtis')	●	●				●	●		●	●	
Columbine (*Aquilegia* 'McKana Giants')	●	●				●	●		●		
Coneflower (*Rudbeckia* 'Goldsturm')	●					●	●		●	●	
Coreopsis (*Coreopsis verticillata* 'Moonbeam')	●					●	●		●	●	
Daylily (*Hemerocallis* 'Stella de Oro')	●					●	●		●	●	
Fountain grass (*Pennisetum alopecuroides*)		●				●	●		●	●	
Goldenrod (*Solidago* 'Golden Wings')	●					●	●		●	●	
Hosta (*Hosta* 'Tattoo')		●				●	●		●	●	
Ligularia (*Ligularia przewalskii*)	●						●		●	●	
Lily (*Lilium* 'White Lace')	●					●	●		●	●	
Michaelmas daisy (*Aster x frikartii* 'Monch')	●					●	●		●	●	
Ostrich fern (*Matteuccia struthiopteris*)		●				●	●		●		

	Light Pastel Flower Color	Light Airy Texture	Vertical Plane Growth	Overhead Plane Foliage	Take to Pruning	Takes Some Crowding	Adapts to Containers	Fine for Pots/Urns	Ground-Level Hardy	Rooftop Hardy	None Hardy	Shade Tolerant
(Perennials, continued)												
Phlox (*Phlox maculata* 'Miss Lingard')							●		●	●		
Striped eulalia grass *(Miscanthus sinensis)*		●				●	●		●	●		
Plume grass (*Erianthus ravennae*)		●				●	●		●	●		
Yarrow (*Achillea* 'Summer Pastels')	●	●				●	●		●	●		
Annuals												
Begonia (*Begonia semperflorens* 'Stara')	●	●				●	●	●			●	●
Coleus (*Coleus blumei* 'Rainbow Mixed')		●				●	●	●			●	●
Cosmea (*Cosmos bipinnatus* 'Sonata')	●	●				●	●	●				
Dahlia (*Dahlia* 'Piccolo')	●					●	●	●				
Dusty miller (*Cineraria* 'Silver Dust')		●				●	●	●				
Geranium (*Pelargonium hortoram* 'Breakaway')	●					●	●	●				
Impatiens (*Impatiens wallerana* 'Accent')	●					●	●	●			●	●
Marigold (*Tagetes* 'Disco Gold')	●					●	●	●				
Petunia (*Petunia hybrida* 'Surfinia White')	●					●	●	●				
Spider flower (*Cleome spinosa* 'Helen Cambell')	●					●	●	●				
Sage (*Salvia splendens* 'Strata')	●					●	●	●				
Tobacco plant (*Nicotiana alata* 'Domino')	●					●	●	●				
Tropicals (as Annuals)												
Australian tree fern (*Dicksonia antarctica*)		●					●				●	●
Bougainvillea (*Bougainvillea* 'Spectabilis')	●		●	●			●				●	
Bower vine (*Pandorea jasminoides*)	●	●	●	●		●	●				●	
Chilean jasmine (*Mandevilla splendens*)	●	●	●	●		●	●				●	
Hibiscus (*Hibiscus* 'Rosasinensis')	●						●				●	
Oleander (*Nerium oleander*)	●						●				●	
Passionflower (*Passiflora caurulea*)	●	●	●	●		●	●				●	
Plumbago (*Plumbago auriculata*)	●	●					●				●	

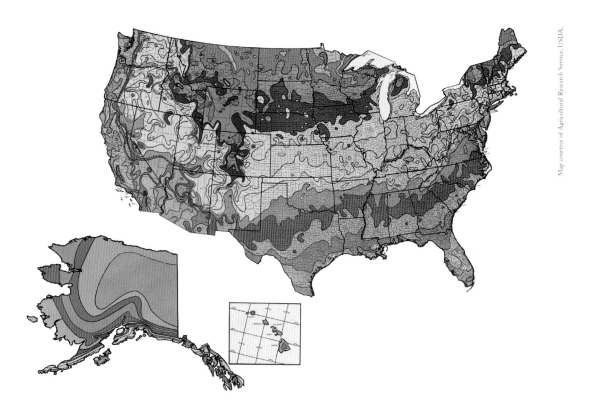

USDA Plant Hardiness Zone Map

The hardiness map was developed by the Agricultural Research Services of the United States Department of Agriculture (USDA). Zones 1–11 are based on the average annual minimum temperature for each zone, with the numbers increasing in warmer climates. The lower the hardiness rating number, the better the chance a plant can survive the winter; the higher the number, the most southerly the area in which it will perform consistently. Many factors—such as altitude, degree of exposure to wind (chill factor and desiccation), reflection from city heat islands (buildings, concrete, etc.), microclimates, loss of ground-moderating effects (planters), proximity to bodies of water, insulating snow cover, and amount of sun exposure—can create variations of as much as two climate zones in winter hardiness.

Average Annual Minimum Temperature		
Temperature (˚C)	Zone	Temperature (˚F)
-45.6 and below	1	Below 50
-42.8 to -45.5	2a	-45 to -50
-40.0 to -42.7	2b	-40 to -45
-37.3 to -40.0	3a	-35 to -40
-34.5 to -37.2	3b	-30 to -35
-31.7 to -34.4	4a	-25 to -30
-28.9 to -31.6	4b	-20 to -25
-26.2 to -28.8	5a	-15 to -20
-23.4 to -26.1	5b	-10 to -15
-20.6 to -23.3	6a	-5 to -10
-17.8 to -20.5	6b	0 to -5
-15.0 to -17.7	7a	5 to 0
-12.3 to -15.0	7b	10 to 5
-9.5 to -12.2	8a	15 to 10
-6.7 to -9.4	8b	20 to 15
-3.9 to -6.6	9a	25 to 20
-1.2 to -3.8	9b	30 to 25
1.6 to -1.1	10a	35 to 30
4.4 to 1.7	10b	40 to 35
4.5 and above	11	40 and above